CHINESE WOMEN AND THE TEACHING PROFESSION

CHINESE WOMEN AND THE TEACHING PROFESSION

JULIA KWONG
AND
MA WANHUA
EDITORS

Nova Science Publishers, Inc.
New York

For permission to use material from this book please contact us:
Telephone 631-231-7269; Fax 631-231-8175
Web Site: http://www.novapublishers.com

NOTICE TO THE READER

The Publisher has taken reasonable care in the preparation of this book, but makes no expressed or implied warranty of any kind and assumes no responsibility for any errors or omissions. No liability is assumed for incidental or consequential damages in connection with or arising out of information contained in this book. The Publisher shall not be liable for any special, consequential, or exemplary damages resulting, in whole or in part, from the readers' use of, or reliance upon, this material. Any parts of this book based on government reports are so indicated and copyright is claimed for those parts to the extent applicable to compilations of such works.

Independent verification should be sought for any data, advice or recommendations contained in this book. In addition, no responsibility is assumed by the publisher for any injury and/or damage to persons or property arising from any methods, products, instructions, ideas or otherwise contained in this publication.

This publication is designed to provide accurate and authoritative information with regard to the subject matter covered herein. It is sold with the clear understanding that the Publisher is not engaged in rendering legal or any other professional services. If legal or any other expert assistance is required, the services of a competent person should be sought. FROM A DECLARATION OF PARTICIPANTS JOINTLY ADOPTED BY A COMMITTEE OF THE AMERICAN BAR ASSOCIATION AND A COMMITTEE OF PUBLISHERS.

LIBRARY OF CONGRESS CATALOGING-IN-PUBLICATION DATA

Available upon request   *1006613055*

ISBN 978-1-59033-916-9

Published by Nova Science Publishers, Inc. ✦ *New York*

CONTENTS

In: Chinese Women and the Teaching Profession
Editors: Julia Kwong and Ma Wanhua

ISBN 978-1-59033-916-9
© 2009 Nova Science Publishers, Inc.

Editors' Introduction

Julia Kwong[1] and Ma Wanhua[2]

[1]The Department of Sociology, the University of Manitoba, Canada
[2]Beijing University, China

This is the last of a three part series on women and education. The first issue (vol. 33, no. 2) addressed women's education and employment, the second (vol. 33, no.3) examined the orientations and attitudes of women students on campus, and the third focuses on the teaching profession, and particularly women teachers in universities. One theme runs through all three issues: women have made tremendous progress since the communist government came to power but they still have many gender-related hurdles to overcome if they are to attain their career goals. Women have more opportunities in higher education and more employment opportunities; but school administrations as well as leaders in work units prefer men to women and impose harsher demands on women. As creatures of this social environment, women's attitudes and psychology to some extent reflect their interior social status, which puts them at further disadvantage. Some do not have high aspirations, have not fully developed their potentials, and lack confidence.

New ideas generally emerge on university campuses. The educational system, especially at the university level, is supposedly the vanguard of social change. Any improvement in women's status should first be reflected there. But the conclusions drawn from the readings in this issue are disappointing. The selections show that educational institutions are not that different from other social institutions even in the treatment of their own staff, and the experiences of women teachers are similar to those in other social sectors.

Selections 1 and 2 document inroads women teachers have made in higher education. They rose from a mere 11 percent of the teaching staff in 1950 to about 20 percent in 1960, and gradually increased to 26 percent in 1977 and 31 percent in 1986. The increase is less impressive when one takes rank into consideration. Women generally permeate the lower ranks. In 1985, only 6 percent of women teachers in higher education nationwide were professors and 13.8 percent were at the associate level. Selection 2 shows that women made further progress in the nineties. Even though the male-female ratio among university staff in 1993 remained constant (at about 2:1), the percentage of women increased to 12 percent at the professorial rank and 22 percent at the rank of associate professor. The picture presented in the third essay is even more optimistic. In Sichuan Province, the proportion of women faculty members matched the national average, but 15.6 percent of the professors and 24 percent of the associate professors were women. Women constituted 40 percent of the technical staff and many won provincial and national awards for their research achievements.

The rate of increase in women teachers is higher at the elementary and secondary levels – to the extent that it has alarmed some academics. Furthermore, the enrollment ratio in teachers training colleges suggests that this trend is likely to remain, as noted in the concluding assay in this issue. The male-female ratio among teachers in elementary and secondary schools was 1:1.5 in the 1990s, an imbalance not as great as the 2:1 ratio in institutions of higher learning. Yet some academics worry about the feminization of teachers in schools and not the masculineness of university staff. They are concerned with the perceived and unproven negative influences that predominantly female teachers may have on the younger generation (see the essays by Fu Songtao and Shi Jinfang). According to these academics, the exposure of the young at a formative stage of their character development to a mainly female teaching staff can lead to a "soft" and effeminate personality even among boys. They become indecisive, weak, complacent, unmotivated, uncompetitive, obedient, uncreative, and conforming - qualities ill-suited to the competitive requirements of the market economy. From the perspective of these members of the teaching profession, the predominance of women would lower their social status. Chinese society is, after all, a patriarchal society: the aggregation of the subordinate gender in a particular profession would lower the remuneration and its status.

Selections 2,3,5,6,8 and 9 examine the reasons for women's lack of success in teaching and research, or in the jargon the authors, their failure to become "talented professional." Since women faculty members have already proven themselves ready to be recruited into the academic ranks by excelling in local and national examinations, their lack of professional achievements cannot be attributed to inferior intellect and ability. The more sympathetic have blamed discriminatory practices on campuses, which have denied women opportunities to learn and to excel. Moreover, all the authors that address this issues attribute the cause in varying degrees to role conflict. Unlike male colleagues who devote all their efforts to their careers, women faculty members divide their attention between family and work. Even though women are accepted into the work force, contemporary Chinese society still expects women to fulfill their traditional role as wife and mother. These expectations pose a dilemma for women and create stress. A few sacrifice family for career; some choose the impossible tasks of balancing between the demands of family and work, but the majority sacrifice their career for their family—with some finding vicarious satisfaction in the success of their husbands and children. As a result, women generally do not excel in job performance, and are slow to rise in their ranks.

In all these essays, there are very few recommendations for change in the expectations of society toward women. The more liberal authors call for giving more opportunities to women, while others suggest improving treatment of teachers as much to attract men to become teachers as to raise the status of women teachers. The most interesting suggestion in these selections perhaps is advocating the study of home economics among women faculty members to make them more "dutiful wives and good mothers." Zhang Xiuqing argues that modern society is making new demands on women academics. They should manage their family as they manage their work and set a schedule for the different tasks at home to better cope with their domestic duties. They should not only look after their children's physical needs, but help them in their mental and emotional development. They should cook nice meals for the family because this is after all a labor of love, and no chef can take their place.

In: Chinese Women and the Teaching Profession
Editors: Julia Kwong and Ma Wanhua

ISBN 978-1-59033-916-9
© 2009 Nova Science Publishers, Inc.

INTRODUCTION

CHINESE WOMEN AND THE TEACHING PROFESSION

As socialization agents, schools are even more powerful than the family in shaping the hearts and minds of the young. Governments use school systems to impart appropriate ideologies and cultures to the next generation. What is taught in a school reflects the values accepted and promoted in society; and what goes on within its walls mirrors the external milieu. School activities are generally carefully planned, organized, and monitored; and trains the young to take up their future roles. Schools, therefore, can be seen as windows through which the society in which they are located can be examined. For this reason, the experience of women teaching or receiving in-service training on the university campuses examined in the selections of this book should be similar to the situation of women in other sectors of Chinese society. Therefore, this book is not only a study of Chinese women in teaching, it also provides readers a glimpse of the situation of women and the attitudes towards women in Chinese society at large.

Within a school system, the university as the highest level in the educational ladder takes on the conflicting but interesting roles as the conveyor of culture on one hand, and the vanguard of change on the other. In the former, it plays a conservative role. Academics have long been socialized in the system, by conforming, being tested and meeting set expectations. Those who have excelled in meeting these expectations are considered cream of the crop, and only the "best" of these are kept on as teachers on campus. In its latter role as a progressive agent of change, the university is not only the place where research is carried out and new knowledge generated, but is also the place where intellectuals young and old gather, criticize what goes on, develop new social ideas, and clamor for change. The thinking and behavior of these women teachers on university campuses not only tell us where women are but also where they may be going.

With the exception of the editor, contributors to this volume are Chinese academics holding positions in Chinese universities. From their vantaged locations, these authors have collected materials, and carried out studies that academics from outside the country may not have been able to do. Their articles are not written for foreign consumption; they have been written for a Chinese audience and published in Chinese journals and magazines between 1993 and 2002. Because their writings do not cater to the expectations and tastes of the West, their analyses and suggestions give readers a rare and authentic glimpse of the different positions taken by Chinese academics on the values and role of Chinese women teachers.

The two articles of Zhang Jianqi document the progress women teachers have made in higher education. Their number rose from a mere 11 percent of the university teaching staff in 1950 to about 20 percent in 1960, and gradually increased to 26 percent in 1977, 31 percent in 1986, and has leveled off since then. Women faculty members as a percentage of the teaching staff almost tripled between 1950s and 1990s. In 1985, about 6 percent of the professors and 13.8 percent of the associate professors across the country were women. In 1993, the percentages increased to 12 percent and 22 percent respectively; and the percentage of women represented in these ranks in some key or prestigious universities are even slightly higher than the national average.

However, these gains made over time are less impressive if we compare the numbers for women with those of their male counterparts - women are still under-represented and constitute a minority in the teaching ranks. Zhang further reminds us that women are concentrated in the lower ranks with over 33 percent and 42 percent women at the lecturer and tutor levels respectively compared to the 12 and 22 percent at the professorial and associate professor levels. Moreover, less than 10 percent of the women teaching in the university have a doctoral degree, and only 20 of the more than 1000 universities in China are headed by women. Pan Houjie reports that women academics are high achievers; they have won various prizes in teaching and research at the national and local levels, but one has no idea if women have been proportionally represented as recipients. Furthermore, if only one of the 6 national laboratories in Sichuan is headed by a woman, this number is certainly below the percentage of women on the teaching staff. Women may be well-represented in the medical field. However, medicine as a discipline does not carry the same prestige as in the West and they are under-represented in the more prestigious disciplines in China, such as, the sciences. The picture of women's participation in institutes of higher education remains a mixed one - the rate of increase in the number of women among university staffs is impressive, but they remain a minority especially in the higher ranks.

Nevertheless, as Zhang has reported, some are worried about this rate of increase in women's participation on campus. University employment is becoming less financially rewarding compared to other fields, such as, business; and attracts larger numbers of women. The unsympathetic are afraid that the continued influx of women will eventually undermine the quality of leadership on campus, but they forget that men (male to female 2:1 ratio) still predominate in institutes of higher education. Others are worried about the preponderance of women in the humanities at the university level, but they overlook that men are in the majority in all other disciplines.

The sex ratio is 1:1.5 among teaching staffs at the elementary and the secondary levels, not as unbalanced as that in the universities. Shi Jinfang reports that in Nantong Normal College, female students constitute more than half of the new students admitted. If enrollment at Nantong Normal College reflects what is going on at other teacher training colleges, the dominance of women teachers at the elementary and secondary levels is likely to continue. This trend alarms some academics in education. They are worried about the "feminization" of teachers in schools at the elementary and secondary levels but do not see the "maleness" of university staff (2:1 sex ratio) as a problem. They are concerned about the perceived negative influences the predominantly female teaching staff may have on the younger generation. According to Fu Zongtao and Shi Jinfang, the exposure of the young at a formative stage of their character development to teaching staff composed mainly of women can lead to a "soft" and effeminate personality even among boys. They become weak, indecisive, cautious, complacent, unmotivated, uncompetitive, obedient, uncreative, and conforming - qualities ascribed to women but deemed negative and ill-suited to the competitive requirements of the market economy. In addition, Fu worries that the dominance of women in the teaching profession could lower the status of the profession. He explains that China after all is a patriarchal and authoritarian society (he does not see that as a problem), and he worries that the aggregation of women, the subordinate gender, in a particular profession would lower the renumeration and its status, and thereby discourage men from becoming teachers.

Many Chinese academics no doubt disagree with this position, but even those sympathetic to women agree with Fu on the central influences of teachers in shaping students' personalities. Coming from the opposite perspective, Li Lihua and Zhang Lili do not see the feminine characteristics of tolerance, caution, or conciliation as negative; but they too see these qualities as not conducive to future success. They worry about the damaging effects teachers promoting these traits may have on students. They argue that teachers too are prisoners of the social culture. As a result, teachers think boys are more intelligent and more creative; and can do better than girls. Because teachers see girls as warm, dependent, and obedient, and boys as outgoing, independent, and strong, they have higher expectations for and more confidence in boys than girls. Moreover, some teachers prefer boys to girls, are more tolerant of boys breaking rules; and give boys more opportunities to develop. And sad to say, Zhang found a larger number of women teachers than men teachers sharing that opinion. The authors warn that the gender bias of the teachers will be transmitted to students in classroom interaction. The Pygmalion effect, identified by Rosenthal, is at play in Chinese society - teachers' expectations become a reality. With teachers' lower expectations for girls than boys, they provide less encouragements and less opportunities to the former to develop than the latter. Girls become dependent, lack confidence and motivation, and do not have a chance to develop their full potential; boys generally have exactly the opposite experience. To Li and Zhang, this explains why girls do not attain the same achievement levels as boys in school, and how the cycle of female incompetence is perpetuated.

This socialization experienced by girls in the early years influences their later lives and explains women's lack of success in teaching and research on university campuses; or in the jargon of Zhou Xin and Huang Xuemei, women's failure to become "talented professionals." Since women faculty members are considered the elites among China's educated class, they have already proved their abilities. Along the way they have surpassed a lot of men by excelling in local and national examinations to enter universities and have done well enough in universities to be invited to stay on as faculty members. Zhou and Huang attribute the scarcity of women in the higher academic ranks to their lack of professional achievements, but they do not believe that this performance or lack of performance can be attributed to inferior intellect or ability.

The more sympathetic, like Pan Houjie, blame the discriminatory practices on campus with university administrations lacking confidence in women, overlooking women in assigning tasks and thus denying them opportunities to prove themselves, to improve, and to excel. Aside from the socially acquired 'feminine' characteristics that work to their disadvantage, these authors without exception attribute in varying degrees women's under achievement to role conflict. Academic work is demanding and requires time and concentration. Unlike male colleagues who devote most if not all their energy and time to their careers, women faculty members have to divide their attention and time between family and work. Even though women are accepted into the work force, contemporary Chinese society still expects women to fulfil their traditional roles as wives and mothers. With the introduction of reform and the market changes since the eighties, the Chinese government have allowed the "law of the market" to take its course. The government retreat from their active role in the provision of social programs and the promotion of social justice including the protection of women's rights. Traditional values die hard, and these values that disadvantaged women once suppressed by the government prior to the reforms re-emerge, and the domestic role of women is once more emphasized in society. Instead of seeing themselves as capable women "holding up half the sky," even college students increasingly seek security in finding a man and see their role as managing the home. Furthermore, in China's still relatively strong extended family system, women not only look after their husbands and children, but their aging parents and their parents-in-law. Consequently, Fan Wan-e found that women engage in a lot more domestic duties, such as, grocery shopping, cooking, doing laundry, and looking after children than men; and they spend twice as much time in housework. These perceived and real conflicting expectations in work and family pose a dilemma for working women and hold them back in their careers.

Women academics, too, subscribe to this traditional idea of women caring for the home. Surveys of women faculty on campuses found that few would sacrifice family for career, over 60 percent chose the almost impossible task of balancing the demands of family and work, and many are willing to sacrifice their careers for family - with some finding vicarious satisfaction in the successes of their husbands and children. Society has different expectations for men and women. Unlike the situation for men, a woman's successful career is not entirely approved of. Some women even avoid success because successful women often encounter misunderstanding, isolation, jealousy, backbiting, and rejection from colleagues and friends. And in some cases, they end up in a divorce. Because of these psychological and social fetters, women are not motivated to achieve even when they have the ability to do so. In fact, many women choose not to excel in their jobs and to rise slowly through their ranks.

These Chinese social scientists have put different emphases on the host of complex and interrelated external and internal variables, structural and psychological factors, societal and individual values, and macro or micro level social organizations that contribute to women's lack of achievement. Sympathetic academics conclude that the roots of most women's lackluster professional achievement are many. Some trace the cause to structural factors, others to societal norms, and still others to women's own psyches; but these factors are all interrelated. Less sympathetic colleagues tend to focus on women's lack of achievement orientation, their misplaced priorities, and poor efforts saying that women have no one but themselves to blame.

In the increasingly competitive market economy, employees no longer hold iron rice bowls or lifetime employment. Employers want to cut cost and layoff or dismiss their employees whenever possible. Job competition is keen, and continued employment and promotion rest not on seniority but on performance. In some sectors, there are calls for "women to go home" or to adopt "phased employment," that is, to stay home when they have children. Such calls are not heard on university campuses, and none of the authors in these selections suggest that women go home. Perhaps this is why some authors argue that discrimination is subtle. But Zhang Xiuqing comes close to making this suggestion. He advocates that a woman faculty member should study home economics to make her a better "dutiful wife and good mother." He argues that since modern society is making new demands on women academics, they should manage their families as they manage their work by setting a schedule for different tasks at home to better cope with their domestic duties. Women should not only look after their husbands' physical needs, they should be their soul mates and provide emotional support. They should not only feed and clothe their children, they should help their mental and emotional development. They should cook nice meals for the family because this is, after all, a labor of love and no chef can match.

Women academics face increasing pressure to perform. Unlike the past when "serving the people" was the ideal, individual success is increasingly valued in contemporary Chinese society and Chinese women too value achievement. But given the very different ideological positions Chinese academics have taken on gender issues, the solutions they pose to resolve women's lack of achievement in the university setting are equally wide ranging. The more liberal academics call for structural changes in the universities to provide more opportunities for women to prove themselves. Others suggest improving working conditions and giving women support in childcare and other domestic duties. The more progressive ones, influenced by the interventionist approach adopted by feminists in the West, propose raising consciousness among teachers. They recommend that 1) exercises be introduced in teacher training programs so that both neophytes and veterans can recognize the gender bias in their views, and discuss strategies to change gender discrimination practised in schools; 2) the curriculum be revised so that the traditional patriarchal views will not be transmitted from generation to generation; 3) more choices and avenues should be provided to young women; 4) young women academics should improve themselves, enroll in postgraduate programs or engage in research; 5) established academics should mentor the young ones to help them learn how to write proposals and carry out research projects so that they can move ahead; and 6) men should be involved in these programs too. They ask women to change their outlook, but not to the extent of abandoning or downplaying their domestic roles. Most advocate restructuring the organization of education to give women and girls greater opportunities for growth, and they exhort women to improve themselves. Only two out of the fourteen authors suggest using affirmative action to re-align the gender imbalance.

If women academics, the elite among women and in society, are facing prejudice and discrimination, less educated and less accomplished women in other walks of life no doubt face more difficulties and have more hurdles to overcome. If academics can so openly profess their patriarchal views in publications, one can surmise that the articulation and manifestation of such thinking are by no means subtle or infrequent in society. If gender bias and discrimination can be so entrenched in universities, putatively more liberal and avant-garde among social institutions, one can imagine that the positions taken by members of other social institutions will be more extreme. If so many men and women academics are still oblivious of the gender bias and discrimination around them, other Chinese men and women will be even more unaware and consciously or unconsciously more receptive of such attitudes and practices.

True, some men and women teachers surveyed by Zhang Lili and Li Lihua have felt that no change is necessary or believe that such imbalance will never be corrected. However, there are also signs of change to come. Universities are after all vanguards and agents of social change. Academics, and mainly women academics, are becoming aware of the problem and beginning to look for solutions. They remain a minority, but a start has been made. These women academics may not be advocating anything earth-shattering in that they do not reject women's domestic role, but they do accept the expanding and conflicting roles women have to play. Few have asked for changes to accommodate the demands of their conflicting roles.

They only ask for structural changes to provide girls and women an equal chance to grow. They have not asked men to change; their attention is on changing and improving themselves. As a first step some want women to be aware of the issues; and consciousness raising is their way of doing it - a strategy adopted by their sisters in the West in the feminist movement of the sixties. Like their sisters in the sixties, these women in China have a long road ahead!

The selections in this volume are divided into six parts. The first part provides an overview of the situation of women in Chinese universities. In the first article, Zhang Jiangqi traces the place of women in the universities since the establishment of the Chinese People's Republic since 1949. In the second article, she compares some of the changes in China with what has happened in other countries, and examines the qualifications and specialties of these university women. Pan Houjie's article focuses on the situation of women academics in one province - Sichuan.   The two articles in Part Two discuss the feminization of the teaching profession. Fu Songtao worries that the women teachers' "rouge and powder" will rub off on the next generation to turn out "effeminate" boys lacking the assertive and competitive spirit required for success in modern China. Shi Jinfang studies the enrolment pattern in a teacher training college in Nantong and is concerned that the predominance of female teachers will continue. Zhou Xin and Huang Xuemei's articles in Part Three confirm the observations in Part One - women academics remain in the junior ranks on campus. To overcome that, Zhou proposes that women should be ambitious, have high aspirations, and participate in research; and society should be more supportive and provide social programs to alleviate women's domestic duties. Huang studies the problem among women of different age groups and again proposes that women should be confident, motivated, and persevering. The three articles in Part Four examine the role conflict faced by women in higher education. Huang Huifang traces the changing role of women from a historical perspective, Liu Jianling examines the gender gaps in contemporary society, and Fan Wen-e explores the internal conflicts faced by women teachers showing that women are still steeped in the traditional cultures governing women's roles. The next section turns to how the traditional ideas held by teachers may affect the young. Zhang Lili and Li Lihua carried out a survey of 110 graduate students enrolled in Beijing Normal Universities. Their findings confirm that women academics still embrace very traditional gender roles. These two authors study classroom interaction to see how the teachers' biased gender attitudes are passed on to the detrimental of women students' development. Most of the authors end their papers with suggestions on how to deal with the problem, but the two papers in the last section provide greater details on these strategies and the solutions proposed reflect the polar opposite positions taken by these academics. Zhang Xiuqing sees the participation of women in academia as undermining their domestic role and advocates a more efficient use of their time so that they can pay more attention to the emotional well-being and development of their husbands and children. Liu Xuanqing and Wan Qionghua, coming from a different perspective, argue that women should be more motivated, confident, and interested in developing their academic abilities. Together the fifteen selections in this book offer readers insight into the very complex situation of and the wide gamut of opinions held by Chinese academics on women in China. Women in China are disadvantaged, but there is a glimmer of hope that things will change.

PART I: SITUATION OF WOMEN TEACHERS

In: Chinese Women and the Teaching Profession
Editors: Julia Kwong and Ma Wanhua

ISBN 978-1-59033-916-9
© 2009 Nova Science Publishers, Inc.

Chapter 1

HISTORICAL EVOLUTION OF WOMEN TEACHERS IN CHINESE HIGHER EDUCATIONAL INSTITUTIONS SINCE 1949[*]

Zhang Jianqi

Zhongshan University, People's Republic of China

Since 1949, Chinese women have made great strides in teaching in higher educational institutions. This is mainly reflected in the rapid numerical increase of women teachers, the increasingly higher percentages they occupy in the total number of teachers in higher education, and the expanding range of disciplines they teach. However, the situation has varied in different periods, and in fact has differed widely. The factors which affected their becoming teachers at that level also differed. We therefore need to make an analysis of the development of women teachers in higher education during different periods after 1949.

FROM 1949-1966: PRE-CULTURAL REVOLUTION YEARS

During this period, there was a rise in the absolute number of women teachers in higher educational institutions and in their ratio to male teachers. The seventeen pre-Cultural Revolution years can actually be divided into two stages. The first ranged from 1950 to 1958, to the period just prior to the Great Leap Forward, when the rise in number and in ratio was relatively rapid. In 1950, the total number of women teachers in regular colleges and universities in the country was 1,900, making up 11 percent of all teachers. By 1957, the number had risen to 14,300, making up 20.4 percent of the total. The second stage ranged from 1958 after the Great Leap Forward to 1966, the eve of the "Great Cultural Revolution," when the situation was rather complicated. The growth of women teachers in higher educational institutions was consistent with the growth in the ranks of teachers as a whole. From 1958 to 1961, the average annual increase [in women teachers] was around 5,000—that of 1960 was 8,800. Their proportion in the total dropped in 1958 and 1959 but rose again in

---

[*] Translation © 2000 M.E. Sharpe, Inc., from the Chinese text. Zhang Jianqi, "1949 nian yilai woguo gaoxiao nujiaoshi duiwude lishi-yanjin," *Jiangsu gaojiao (Nanjing)* (Jiangsu Higher Education [Nanjing]), 2.72-75 (1997), reprinted in Gaodeng jiaoyu (Higher Education), 6-93 to 6-96.

1961 to 21.2 percent, the highest of all years before the Cultural Revolution. From 1961 to 1965, the total number showed a downturn, as did the proportion of women teachers. However, the proportion remained relatively stable, and at its lowest point (1965), was still 20.8 percent.

A major factor affecting women's entry into the teaching field during this period was the state of higher education itself. From 1950 to 1957, regular higher education developed at a steady and slow pace, as did the increase in the number of women teachers. The Great Leap Forward beginning in 1958 also brought about considerable development in higher education. The number of teachers in regular colleges and universities more than doubled, increasing from 70,000 in 1957 to 158,800 in 1961. The rise in women teachers followed suit. Beginning in the 1960s, the negative consequences of the blind spurt in higher education began to be felt. In addition, the Chinese economy worsened and graduates had trouble finding jobs. Some schools merged, some stopped operating, and others closed down. The ranks of teachers in higher education shrank correspondingly. The number of women teachers in the field dropped from 1962 to 1965.

However, the absolute number of women teachers in higher education was not consistent with the changes in the male-female teacher ratio. Other factors affected women's participation. From 1950 to 1957, the major factor that led to women's proportional increase was that widespread women's employment (including in colleges and universities) was gradually being accepted and approved in the public mindset and popular media had higher expectations of women's social achievement (especially intellectual women). There was also a relaxing of past hiring restrictions by colleges and universities against women—such as that a husband and wife could not be hired at the same school (resulting in the wife often giving up the chance)—which gave women more opportunities to work in higher education. At the same time, during this period there was a relatively abundant source of women teachers, which also brought up their proportion. There were three sources: First women students who had been studying abroad before the founding of the People's Republic now returned. These included Professor Xie Xide of Fudan University, Professor Gao Xiaoxia of Beijing University, and Professor Shen Tianhui of Shanghai's Jiaotong University, who are all members of the Chinese Academy of Sciences. A second source was women college graduates of the past, and the third source was women college graduates educated after the founding of the People's Republic of China. During the second stage, the proportion of women teachers in higher education was relatively stable. The main reason was that the major source had changed to women college graduates and postgraduate students that China itself had educated, as well as some postgraduate students educated abroad. At this time, Chinese women were at a disadvantage in taking higher education, and this partially decided the situation of women teachers in higher education. When there was a shrinking of the scale of higher education, because of the different percentages of cuts in men and women, the proportion of women in the total number dropped from 21.2 percent in 1961 to 20.8 percent in 1965. Another part of the reason was early retirement (at 45) taken by women. During this period, some education policies (such as the abolition of regular women's colleges and universities, the policy of colleges and universities opening their doors to workers and peasants, the vigorous promotion of science and engineering disciplines, etc.) also affected women becoming teachers in higher education.

After the abolition of regular women's colleges and universities, women teachers scattered widely to different places, but in all coed universities and colleges they enjoyed no advantage in numbers or in position. Former presidents of women's colleges and universities lost their positions. This might have been one of the major reasons there were no women university presidents in this period. The policy of opening the doors to workers and peasants brought a relative increase in the number of women college students from worker or peasant origin. Some of them were a major source of women teachers during this time. This was a change from the pre-1949 situation, when the majority of women university and college teachers came from the upper or middle strata of society.

The vigorous promotion of science and engineering disciplines played a big role in widening the distribution of women teachers in different disciplines. The sharp increase in students in science and engineering majors and the quick rise in the proportion of women students in these fields meant a much bigger number of women science and engineering students, which, in turn, produced greater numbers of women teachers in these disciplines. The demand for teachers in these fields also caused more women to become teachers. The vigorous promotion of science and engineering disciplines has had a great impact on the distribution of women teachers in the different disciplines.

Forming a strong contrast with the rapid rise in the ratio of women to men teachers was the large gender gap in presidents and vice presidents of universities and colleges. A few women were appointed vice presidents, but there were no women presidents. China is a country that places a lot of stress on power and position. The fact that males occupied a very high proportion of university president and vice president positions while women barely had any reflects the dominant position of males among the teaching staff of higher educational institutions.

FROM 1966 TO 1975: THE PERIOD
OF THE "GREAT CULTURAL REVOLUTION"

The total number of teachers in higher education dropped during this period. In 1973 and 1974, the number was 132,000 and 134,400, respectively, both lower than that in 1966. The numbers went back up in 1975 and 1976. However, in this period and especially beginning in 1973, the proportion of women to the total number of teachers in higher education showed a rising trend. The number of women teachers in higher education was 30,000 in 1973, 31,600 in 1974, 38,000 in 1975, and 41,300 in 1976, making up 22.7 percent, 23.5 percent, 24.4 percent, and 24.7 percent of the total, respectively. The reason for this might have been the fact that there were relatively fewer women among the targets of struggle and criticism of that time, the "capitalist roaders" and "Bourgeois academic authorities." As a result, a smaller number of women teachers in higher education was hit as compared to men. At the same time, the proportion of graduates from women's colleges and universities was relatively high, providing a bigger source for the contingent of teachers in higher education. In addition, there was an unprecedented social environment for gender equality, which also removed many of the conceptual obstacles to women's participation in the higher education teaching ranks.

During this period, the work to determine and elevate the professional titles of teachers came to a halt. Newcomers were generally made assistant professors or had no fixed titles. With the rise in the proportion of women teachers, their proportions in assistant professors and teachers also rose. The cessation of the work of conferring titles and promoting teachers to higher titles had a larger negative effect on women teachers in higher education and, in fact, lessened their opportunity to get higher titles.

FROM 1977 TO THE PRESENT: A PERIOD OF REFORM AND OPENING

During this period, the trend has been a rising one whether in the number of women teachers in higher education or in their ratio to male teachers. Again, we can divide the period into two stages. The first is from 1977 to 1985. The number of women teachers rose rapidly, but in proportion to male teachers the situation was sluggish or even registered a slight drop. In 1977, full-time women teachers in regular colleges and universities in the nation numbered 49,900, or 26.8 percent of the total number of teachers at this level. In 1985, there were 91,900, or 26.7 percent of the total. The second stage was from 1986 to 1993. This period saw a rise both in numbers and in the gender ratio. In 1986, there were 107,100 full-time women teachers in higher education, or 30.9 percent of the total. The proportion of women teachers was close to the proportion of women who were receiving education. However, the numerical increase was relatively slow while the proportion rose relatively quickly.

During this period, a significant factor bearing on women's entry into higher education teaching was the development of higher education in China. From 1977 to 1985, the number of new admissions grew annually by a large margin. There was an urgent demand for teachers and the total number of women teachers grew relatively fast. In 1977, the total number of teachers was 186,500, but by 1985, the number had grown to 344,300, or nearly doubled and that resulted in the umber of women teachers in higher education growing correspondingly fast. From 1986 to the present, the growth in the number of higher educational institutions slowed down, increasing from 1,016 in 1986 to 1,065 in 1993. Hence, the total number of teachers did not grow much – in 1986, the figure was 372,400, and in 1993, 387,800 – and neither did the number of women teachers.

However, during this period changes in the number of women teachers in higher education and in the gender ratio were not consistent. Factors affecting women teachers were complicated. From 1977 to 1985, the rise in the proportion of women teachers in the total stopped temporarily, and even dropped. This was not only due to the influence of the "Great Cultural Revolution" but also to other restricting factors. A major work of this period was to "reverse bogus cases and mistaken cases in which people were wronged, and implement the policy toward intellectuals." Many teachers who had stopped teaching or research due to political reasons returned to work in colleges and universities. Because of the higher proportion of male teachers involved, they also returned to work in larger numbers. At the same time, a smaller proportion for women were receiving higher education, especially postgraduate education, while college and university teachers were drawn increasingly from among postgraduates as opposed to college or specialized school graduates. This is a direct and major cause of the low proportion of women teachers in higher education. In addition, with the introduction of competition in hiring and the practice of basing wage and promotion on seniority, egalitarianism broke down and some schools began to refuse or use fewer women graduates.[1] The reasons for this were: during this period the "eating from the same

---

[1] "The Hiring System—Feedback from Women Intellectuals and Counter-Measures," Zhongguo funu (Chinese Women), no. 9, 1988.

pot" system had just been abolished, women found it hard to adjust, and the evaluation of women's accomplishments was at a low ebb. Gender discrimination and prejudice formed over a long period also played a part.

However, after 1986 the number of women teachers in higher education grew slowly, while their proportion in the total rose quickly. The reason was mainly that more women were receiving higher education, especially postgraduate education. There was also an erosion of teachers in higher education. Higher education is education at the highest levels, and the fostering of high-class specialized talent can only be done by teachers with the highest qualifications. The structure of the credentials necessary for obtaining a teaching job in colleges and universities has recently evolved toward higher standards. The fact that more women are receiving postgraduate education has increased their competitiveness in getting college or university teaching jobs. Moreover, erosion in the ranks of teachers began at this time and it was worse among men than women. From 1989 to 1993, the number of full-time teachers in higher educational institutions showed a downturn. The number in 1989 was 397,400 and in 1993 was 387,800. Aside from natural attrition, a major reason was that teachers were taking up new employment. Hence both the number of college and university women teachers and their proportion in the total increased.

After reform and opening, the change in the social environment increased pressure on the social role of women. On campus, competition among teachers in scientific research and academia increased sharply. While society might have different expectations of social roles for men and women, it has the same expectations in terms of job competency for both sexes. The introduction of competition did not bring about the same effects on male and female teachers; women were in a weaker position. The main reason for this is that they were in a weaker position in scientific research, and they had a conflict between their dual roles. Generally speaking, most women teachers were as qualified and competent on the job as men, although there was a considerable difference between male and female teachers with respect to scientific research. The gender difference is pretty obvious in scientific research, and the greater the difficulty of the project, the bigger the difference. For instance, the number of women becomes smaller in reverse proportion to the significance of research findings and awards, far smaller than what the proportion should be.[2] In recent years, our colleges and universities have also started to some extent to develop toward the direction of "putting science research above teaching." Hence, teaching is frequently regarded as a "soft target" of promotions and appointments and scientific research the "hard target," putting a sizable number of women at a disadvantage. In cases of "exceptional" promotions, the importance attached to scientific research has benefited male teachers because of their greater participation in scientific research. Their proportion is thus much higher than for women. Correspondingly, male teachers earn senior ranks at a younger age. To take the example of graduate supervisors, in 1993 women graduate supervisors under thirty years of age were only 2.1 percent of the total and those between thirty-one and forty-five made up 4.2 percent of the total, much lower than the actual proportion of 14.1 percent of women mentors in the total.[3] The proportion of women teachers who received senior ranks or higher management positions, and thus display their talents more fully, is much lower than their proportion in the

---

[2] Huang Qinghua, "Analysis of the Role of Intellectual Women in One University" (paper presented at the international symposium "Role Conflict of Modern Professional Women," October 26-28,1993).

[3] Zhongguo funu jiaoyu (Chinese Women's Education), Table 24.

total number of teachers. Thus, a relatively large number of women teachers in higher education acutely feel the pressure of their social role. They must actively compete in scientific research and academic work and get professional results comparable to the men's before they can feel a sense of achievement and get opportunities for promotions. Their societal role thus vies for time with their family roles. In recent years, the resumption and reinforcement of the social division of work in the family (men take care of matters outside the home and women inside the home), interwoven with fierce competition in scientific research and the academic field, has affected some women and made them feel that it is very hard to be successful in their careers. They withdraw before this new challenge and give up or lower their achievement goals, being satisfied with their low rank and position. All of these factors have affected their participation in higher education.

However, women's status and functions have not, as predicted by some people, entered a "low valley" along with the overall introduction of the competition mechanism.[4] Besides the greater number of women who seek to become teachers in higher education (because more women have received graduate education, and because employment in other areas is even harder to find), the erosion of college and university teachers is also a major reason. Among the young and middle-aged teachers who have left higher education in recent years, a larger proportion were men, while a higher proportion of women among new college graduates take up teaching. Teaching is relatively attractive for women mainly because the flexible work schedules alleviate the conflict between career and home, and this is hard to do in other occupations. The relative stability of college teaching jobs are naturally more attractive to intellectual women who are not willing to take risks and compete strenuously. [*] Society generally views teaching in higher education as a good choice for women, although the same is not true of men. This social concept has affected women's and men's choices to some extent. Discrimination against women in the employment market makes it difficult for young and middle-aged women teachers to go into other occupations and also for new women graduates to get highly paid jobs. This forces some of them to retreat and take the second best. In talent exchange, the advantage formerly enjoyed by higher educational institutions as the "buyer" have gradually eroded; they have to take more women college graduates even if they do not like it. All this has brought about an increase in the number and proportion of women teachers in higher education. This phenomenon is especially marked in certain disciplines and has caused some researchers to appeal for greater attention to teachers in higher education, especially the question of the "feminizing" of the liberal arts disciplines.[5]

In evaluating the progress of Chinese women teaching in the higher educational field, we should also take a look at their ranks and administrative positions. In recent years, the proportion of women with higher ranks has increased. In 1985, the number of women with the title of professor and associate professor was 300 and 400, respectively, making up 6 percent and 13.8 percent of the total numbers. In 1992, the numbers were 2,000 and 1,800, respectively, occupying 10.5 percent and 20.9 percent of the total. The proportion of women

---

[4] Wang Hongwei, "Analysis of Women Intellectuals of Wuhan Higher Educational Institutions in Competition," Zhongguo funu fencing yanjiu (Stratified Analysis of Chinese Women) (Henan People's Publishing House, n.d.), pp. 199-211.

[*] Although the teaching profession since the Cultural Revolution has become more strenuous, it still is not as competitive as other professions.—Ed.

[5] Liu Xiaoming et al., "Exploration and Analysis of the 'Feminizing' of Liberal Arts Teachers in Higher Educational Institutions," Guangming ribao (Guangming Daily), December 13,1995.

with higher ranks is increasing in numbers and relative to men. Moreover, there has also been progress in higher administrative positions. Most significant is the fact that some women have served as presidents of universities (e.g., Xie Xide, president of Fudan University; Wei Jue, president of the Southeastern University; Wu Qidi, president of Tongji University; Zheng Shu, president of the Zhejiang School of Medicine; Hua Jingjuan, president of the Wuxi Light Industry Institute (now called the Wuxi Light Industry University); Cai Lan, president of the Jiangsu Science and Engineering University; etc.) What is notable is that they have headed some of the top universities in our country. The above-mentioned all came from science, engineering, or medical education backgrounds, and most have studied abroad. From a geographical point of view, they are concentrated in Jiangsu, Zhejiang, and Shanghai. This may have to do with the fact that the women in this area are relatively well educated and have a strong ability for civic participation, and people here are more receptive to women becoming leaders of colleges and universities.

Since 1949, there has been a significant expansion of the contingent of women teachers in Chinese higher education. This is closely connected with the rise in women's economic and political position. The expansion of the scale of higher education and its teaching staff has provided the opportunity for women to enter its ranks. The fact that more Chinese women are able to receive higher education has also made it possible for women to become teachers in higher education. After reform and opening, new changes and factors of influence have appeared in this area. However, although much progress has been made, the progress is not satisfactory. Therefore, further improving the situation is an important and arduous task. It needs both the support of the government and higher education administration, as well as the efforts of Chinese women teachers in higher education.

(Editor-in-charge: Gu Guanhua)

In: Chinese Women and the Teaching Profession
Editors: Julia Kwong and Ma Wanhua

ISBN 978-1-59033-916-9
© 2009 Nova Science Publishers, Inc.

Chapter 2

STUDY OF THE STATUS OF WOMEN TEACHERS IN CHINA'S HIGHER EDUCATION[*]

Zhang Jianqi

After the founding of the People's Republic of China, as major progress was made in women's participation in higher education, the proportion of women teachers in higher educational institutions gradually increased and their status has significantly improved. What, then, is the status of women teachers in China's higher education today? This is an issue which still deserves our exploration. Thus, let us first do our best to reflect on this status relatively accurately. In this article, the status of women teachers is a relative concept and is used in reference to and comparison with male teachers' status. At the same time, the status of women teachers is a collective concept, including primarily the proportion of women teachers to the total number of teachers in present-day regular universities and colleges, the distribution of their disciplines, their entry into faculties of universities and colleges, their promotion in title and rank, and their self-cognition and social identity.

PROPORTION OF WOMEN TEACHERS

With more women receiving higher education after the founding of the People's Republic, the development of higher education and women's employment (including teaching in institutes of higher learning) has been widely accepted in society. The proportion of women teachers in higher education has risen greatly and the gender gap is narrow. The rate of increase in the number of female teachers is much higher than that of female college students, but the percentage is still much lower than male teachers. Taking 1993 ни example, the ratio of male to female teachers was 69.1:30.9. That is, for every 100 male teachers in colleges and universities, there were only 45 female teachers. The gender gap in this area, however, is not that wide when compared to other countries. In Belgium, for instance, the proportion of women teachers in universities and colleges in 1989 was around 43 percent,

---

[*] Translation © 2000 M.E. Sharpe, Inc., from the Chinese text. Zhang Jianqi, "Woguo gaoxiao nujiaoshi diwei xianzhuang zhi yanjiu," *Qinghua daxuejiaoyu yanjiu* (Research on Education, Qinghua University), no. 4, 1997. Zhang Jianqi is a lecturer at the Institute of Higher Education, Zhongshan University, Guangzhou.

while in Finland in 1989, the proportion of male teachers was 90 percent. The gender gap in our country belongs to the middle level in the world.

The main question at present is that the higher the rank or position, the lower the number of female teachers compared to male counterparts: their number at the different levels clearly forms into the shape of a pyramid. Again taking 1993 as example, full-time women teachers in regular institutions of higher learning made up 30.9 percent of the total number of teachers. The proportions of women with each of the following titles: professors, associate professors, lecturers, tutors, and instructors were, respectively, 12.01 percent, 21.93 percent, 32.89 percent, 41.38 percent, and 36.93 percent.[1] The numbers were actually in inverse ratio: that is, the lower the level, the bigger the numbers—as reflected, for instance, in the large proportion of female tutors and lecturers—and the higher the level, the smaller the number, as among professors. There is a particularly large gender gap among supervisors of Ph.D. students. Women are even more rare among the highest level of education administrators. The number of women who are presidents of universities or heads of institutions at that level is a mere handful. According to statistics, of the over 1,000 regular universities and colleges in the nation, only approximately 20 women are president or vice president, making up an extremely low proportion. Of the 20-odd, more are vice presidents than presidents. Wu Qidi, president of Tongji University, and Cheng Shu, president of the Zhejiang Medical University, are most probably the only two women university presidents in the country. This makes up a little more than one/ one-thousandth of the total. The number is so negligible that women can hardly be said to exist at the highest level of education administration. Compared to other countries, the proportion of women among Chinese university presidents (and vice presidents) is also relatively low. For instance, in 1990, women made up 11.8 percent of university presidents in the United States.[2] Even in Japan, where there is a certain amount of discrimination against women teaching in higher education, the proportions of women among university presidents and other leaders on campus were 0.3 percent and 0.7 percent, respectively, in 1988.[3] However, one factor that needs to be noted is that in many countries women are generally the presidents of women's colleges, whereas in China there are no women's colleges, and hence fewer opportunities for women to be president.

DISCIPLINE DISTRIBUTION OF WOMEN TEACHERS IN HIGHER EDUCATION

Due to the lack of national statistics on the proportion of women teachers in different disciplines in higher education, we can only base our analyses roughly on recent surveys of the specialties of women college students and the situation of full-time teachers in the different disciplines.

According to a survey carried out in 1987, there were a total of 17,987 professors teaching and doing scientific research in regular colleges and universities. Of this, 1,571 were women, making up 9.2 percent of the total. These female professors were distributed in

---

[1] Zhongguo funu jiaoyu (Chinese Women's Education), n.d., p. 20, table.

[2] Guowai gaodeng jiaoyu kuaixun (Newsletter on Higher Education Abroad), edited by the Higher Education Institute of Beijing University, no. 1, January 1994.

[3] Zhongguo funu jiaoyu, n.d., p. 453.

different disciplines: medicine, 20 percent; agriculture, 11 percent; literature and art, 8.2 percent; education, 7.6 percent; science, 7.6 percent; economics, 4.8 percent; history, 4.4 percent; philosophy, 3.6 percent; engineering, 3.3 percent; and law, 1.6 percent. This shows that the proportion of women professors in medicine and agriculture was higher than the average of 9.2 percent, while in other disciplines the proportions were lower than average. The lowest proportion was in law, at only 1.6 percent. Among the female faculty members, 811, or 52 percent, were in medicine; 13.9 percent in science; 10.5 percent in engineering; 9.2 percent in literature and art; 7.1 percent in agriculture; 2.5 percent in economics; 2.4 percent in education; 1.3 percent in history; 0.6 percent in philosophy; and 0.4 percent in law.[4] With respect to the number of women professors, the largest numbers were in medicine, science, and engineering. Among the different disciplines, however, the largest proportion of women professors were found in the medical and agricultural faculties. What should be noted here is that women professors occupy an important place in medicine—whether in numbers or in their proportion in this discipline. Compared with male professors, women professors were to a large extent concentrated in medicine. The situation was more complicated in engineering. Although there were as many as 160 or more women professors in the field, their proportion among the total was relatively low, at only 3.3 percent. The main reason for this was that at the time, China already had a large number of teachers in engineering, including professors (some 5,000).

The distribution of women professors in the various disciplines basically reflected the distribution of women teachers as a whole. Although the proportion occupied by women professors in the various disciplines were not the same, generally speaking the greater the number of teachers in a discipline, the greater the number of professors. In addition, because the proportion of women teachers to the total number of teachers was 27.8 percent, which was far higher than the 9.2 percent of women professors in the total number of professors, the proportion of women teachers in different disciplines was still higher.

In recent years, along with the restructuring in the areas of specialization, the distribution of teachers in the disciplines has also changed. Basically, the number of teachers in the liberal arts, finance, and economics has increased, while the science, engineering, and medical majors still have a great number of teachers. For instance, in 1981 there were 69,753 teachers in engineering, 59,783 in science, 20,011 in liberal arts, 24,321 in medicine, and 4,951 in finance and economics, making up, respectively, 28.4 percent, 24.4 percent, 21.2 percent, 9.9 percent, and 2 percent of the total number of teachers.[5] By 1993, the total number of teachers stood at 107,166 in engineering, 76,827 in science, 87,692 in liberal arts, 33,950 in medicine, and 19,633 in finance and economics, the respective percentages of the total number of teachers being 27.6 percent, 19.3 percent, 22.6 percent, 8.8 percent and 5.1 percent.[6] This shows an increase in the proportion of teachers in the liberal arts, and especially in finance and economics, and a decrease in those of engineering, science, and medicine. This change in the distribution of the disciplines of teachers is correspondingly reflected in the distribution of women teachers. To some extent, more women teachers have turned to liberal arts, finance, and economics.

---

[4] Wu Haiqing, "The Current Status of Female Professors in China Women and Education in China" (Hong Kong and Taiwan, 1990).

[5] Zhongguo jiaoyu nianjian (Chinese Education Yearbook), 1949—81, p. 973.

[6] Zhongguo jiaoyu shiye tongji nianjian (Chinese Education Statistics Yearbook), 1993, p. 26.

Another major factor leading to the change in the distribution of areas of specialization among women teachers in this period is the change in the choice of specialties of women college students. During this period, the latter's choices to some extent have turned to liberal arts, which brought a corresponding rise in women teachers in that area. A 1995 survey of teachers in (he humanities at science and engineering colleges demonstrated this trend. Of the forty-three science and engineering colleges in Beijing (not including eight newly built ones), the total number of teachers in the humanities was 3,622, of which 1,587 were males and 2,055 were females. With respect to changes in teachers as a whole, male teachers under 35 years of age increased 3.16 times as compared with those over 56 (80:371), while the increase for females was 9.13 times in the same age groups (118 : 130). There were more women teachers in the humanities, where the male to female ratio was 43.3:56.7. This was especially so among women teachers under 35, where the male to female ratio was 33.6 : 64.4.[7] Although this survey was conducted among humanities teachers in science and engineering colleges in Beijing, we can still see the trend of increasing numbers of women teachers in the liberal arts.

WOMEN ENTERING HIGHER EDUCATION TEACHING AND PROMOTION IN RANK AND POSITION

The trend in recent years is a gradual increase in women teachers in higher educational institutions. There is a higher proportion of women entering the ranks of teachers, and many have been promoted to higher ranks and office. However, there are still problems as far as their participation in higher education is concerned. The main problem is in the large gender gap favoring males in certain disciplines, with women teachers in rank and office at the lower levels.

This is not to say that women have no problem entering the ranks of teachers. The fact that female college graduates have difficulty finding employment is not entirely caused by the relative discrimination against hiring women in other occupations; colleges and universities prefer males to females in hiring outstanding graduates or filling vacancies in teaching staff. This was especially obvious at the time when the hiring system in institutions of higher learning was first established (particularly in the mid-1980s). A survey by the Shanghai Municipal Women's Federation in 1986, for instance, revealed that some hiring units in Shanghai (including higher educational institutions) did not want or wanted fewer women graduates and researchers, making the researchers worry that the number of women intellectuals in those units (including higher educational institutions) would drop.[8] However, because a college position has lost its luster in recent years, colleges and universities have a smaller pool of outstanding graduates to choose from, and women's opportunities to become teachers in higher education have increased. For some people who discriminate strongly against women, they have no other choice but to allow women to become teachers. The reason is that they feel that an excessive number of women teachers (in 1993, the proportion of women teachers in higher education was 30.9 percent, which they already thought too

---

[7] Liu Xiaoming et al., "Exploration of the Feminization of Liberal Arts Teachers in Institutes of Higher Learning."

[8] "The Appointment System: Feedback from Women Intellectuals in Higher Educational Institutions and Measure Recommended," Zhongguo funu (Chinese Women), no. 9, 1988.

high) will lead to a lack of academic leadership to create an appropriate intellectual structure to accommodate the different personalities and qualities of teachers and in the education of students.[9] Their prejudice against women teachers is very obvious, although they try to cover it up with seemingly reasonable pretexts. When there were few or virtually no women teachers working in higher education, they would think the scarcity was caused by women's lack of qualification to teach in college; they would not ask for more women teachers to be hired to create a reasonable intellectual structure to complement teachers of different personalities and characters. It can be foreseen that once college teaching becomes a sought after position, discrimination against women teachers will only intensify.

The reason for the low rank and office of women teachers can at least partially be attributed to the educational opportunities available to them. The opportunities available have an obvious effect on their future status as teachers. The unfavorable conditions women faced in higher education, especially at the graduate level, determined their status. In 1993, there was a total of 90,717 full-time teachers with graduate training in regular colleges and universities. Of these, 20,139, or 22.2 percent, were women. Those with undergraduate degrees numbered 266,292, of which 90,283 were women, making up 33.9 percent. It can thus be seen that the proportion of women teachers in higher education who had received undergraduate degrees was larger than those who had received graduate education. The proportion of women with Ph.D., master's, and bachelor's degrees were, respectively, 8.61 percent, 23.24 percent, and 37.93 percent of teachers with equivalent degrees.[10] "That is to say, the higher the educational credentials, the fewer the number of women teachers. Although the majority of women college teachers in China has at least a bachelor's degree, the proportion with higher credentials is not high. In comparison, a Ph.D. is a prerequisite to teach in colleges and universities in other countries of the world. This is especially so in world-class universities, where most teachers are required to have a Ph.D. Higher education is education at the highest level. The training of high-level specialists can only be done by teachers with the highest credentials. The credentials of Chinese college and university teachers are developing toward a higher level. Hence, women teachers' lower educational credentials often make it hard for them to be placed in favorable positions. If they were put in favorable positions, they would naturally gain certain advantages that come with these positions. Some women teachers are put in unfavorable positions as soon as they join a higher educational institution, making it very difficult for them to gain outstanding accomplishments and obtain promotions in rank and office. Low credentials also create a widening gap between male and female teachers because many colleges and universities provide different conditions for teachers with different credentials. To attract talented teachers, some universities, for example, provide teachers with a Ph.D. degree with a Scientific Research Initiation fund. Since only 8.16 percent of teachers with Ph.D. degrees are women, they have a much slimmer chance of obtaining this fund.

Another partial explanation for the low level of women teachers' rank and office is their relative weakness in scientific research. This weakness is a major cause of their failure to get promotions. In recent years, Chinese universities have been developing more toward the direction of "putting scientific research first and teaching second" and have imposed strict and

---

[9] Liu Xiaoming et al., "Exploration of the Feminization of Liberal Arts Teachers in Institutes of Higher Learning."
[10] Zhongguo funu jiaoyu (Chinese Women's Education, 1993), table 21 on the credentials of full-time women teachers in regular colleges and universities in China.

high demands on teachers in research. In evaluation, the weight put on scientific research findings is higher. Furthermore, great emphasis is put on a teacher's research ability in decisions regarding promotion. For example, both research accomplishments and managerial ability count in the appointment of university presidents. The majority of women teachers do not have an advantage in these two areas. Therefore, some teachers must change their focus and actively participate in research, or their evaluations will remain low. This will, in turn, further increase their social pressures and affect self-evaluation of their research ability. Besides the lack of attention to research, another reason for the relatively small number of research findings made by women teachers is their low level of participation in school management. This results in a lack of opportunities to nurture managerial talent of the majority of women teachers. But managerial talent and research results are, to some extent, related. Major research projects are frequently the results of collective effort: this requires researcher ability as well as the ability to organize people and use their strengths. This lack of managerial ability in women makes them lag behind men in research—which affects their promotion. This is a vicious cycle.

Of all the obstacles lying in the path of the promotion of women teachers, gender discrimination and prejudice are no doubt the most powerful. The higher success rate of men and the resulting social attitudes also affect higher education. Career success is often regarded as the prerogative of male teachers. Some people in higher education, affected by this social attitude, fail to give women teachers equal opportunity to develop their talent. As a result, women teachers are often placed in unfavorable positions, thus weakening or even completely depriving them of a chance to succeed. Women teachers are also given fewer opportunities to study abroad or to engage in advanced training as compared with men, thus restricting their development. Sometimes gender prejudice leads to this mindset. Because so few women are seen at the higher levels of leadership in colleges and universities, they are overlooked when appointments are considered.

Currently, higher educational institutions discriminate against women teachers not only in promotion, but also in retirement. There has long been a rule that women teachers must retire at age 55. Although the intention might have been to protect their interests, the system not only does not protect their legal rights, but actually restricts their full development. Forced to retire five years earlier than their male counterparts, women teachers are actually deprived of five years of effective competition. Women of this age group possess rich experience in their fields, show more maturity in their work, and get more results in research. For this reason, the country in recent years has clearly provided that "high-ranking female specialists whose physical condition allows them to work can retire at age 60, if they so choose." Some higher educational institutions, however, have imposed the condition "if truly required by work," and apply this clause only to "outstanding specialists at a national level, supervisors of Ph.D. and Master's degree students, leaders of important disciplines, and heads of research projects at the national, provincial, or ministerial levels." This restricts the options of associate women professors and maintains de facto women's retirement at 55. This obvious gender discrimination reflects gender inequality and results in women teachers in higher education retiring five years earlier than male teachers, depriving them of their right to work for the last five years. This no doubt forces women teachers to participate in competition under unfair conditions with leaching and research opportunities that are not equal to those of men. After reaching 45, some women teachers without outstanding accomplishments believe along with other people that their "best years are gone" and lower their career expectations.

At 50, they are regarded as virtual retirees. All this, by and large, determines that women teachers face much greater obstacles and difficulties in getting results in research and in obtaining a higher rank. This is also one of the reasons that the higher the title, the fewer the women teachers who can attain it.

Gender prejudice affects women teachers. Some women teachers may not recognize their own ability, are not enthusiastic about getting higher rank and position, lack a sense of participation, and lose many opportunities to develop themselves and show their talent. As a result, they are not highly regarded. This is tantamount to voluntarily relinquishing the opportunity for professional advancement. This may also be due to the consideration that their opportunity for advancement is less than that of male teachers, and thus make them lose confidence in pursuing it.

In recent years, the number of women teachers in China's higher educational institutions has increased. Generally speaking, people believe teaching at colleges and universities to be a relatively good career choice for women. This belief is shared by many female college students. The reason is that in the eyes of many, colleges and universities have the highest level of culture in society, are open-minded, and are less discriminatory against women. Women therefore have the chance to advance to higher positions. The facts, however, are not so. Chinese colleges and universities are fixated on the practice of overlooking women. In important research projects or in teaching arrangements, women teachers are mostly given secondary roles or considered assistants with few opportunities to work independently. Generally speaking, this problem is most conspicuous in research. Not only are there fewer numbers of women in research, but the number of women heading major projects is even smaller. The situations of women teachers in promotion are worse than male teachers: the opportunity is far from equal.

SELF-COGNITION AND SOCIAL IDENTITY OF WOMEN TEACHERS IN HIGHER EDUCATION

Self-Cognition of Women Teachers in Higher Education

Let us look primarily at female teachers' evaluation of their own ability and their sense of career achievement, and compare these with that of the male teachers.

Generally, women who become teachers in colleges and universities are outstanding college graduates with high evaluations of their own ability. The reasons are that, first, during the long course of study, their high academic achievements (on par with male students) imbued them with self-confidence. They generally feel they are not inferior to male students in the knowledge of their specialties or intellect. Second, a fine education fostered their critical ability, so that they are less liable to accept social prejudices against women. A survey carried out among the female faculty and other staff members of Beijing University showed that women intellectuals shared a common view of their intelligence and talent. They felt that the two genders had different interests. There was no congenital disparity between the sexes: with effort, both can be successful. Of the women surveyed, 91.1 percent held this opinion. Questionnaires sent out during the survey clearly showed the female respondents' evaluated highly their own qualities and abilities: 64.4 percent felt they had an excellent intellect and other natural endowments, and that with effort they were entirely capable of doing well in their jobs; 43 percent were happy with their own career achievements; 25.3 percent felt that their potential had not yet been fully realized and were not very happy with the results of their work. Only 5.2 percent felt that because their ability was limited they were not able to obtain satisfactory results in work. This figure was actually 3.6 percent lower than those who claimed they were satisfied with their careers and had obtained great achievements.[11]

Despite the women teachers' high evaluation of their own abilities (as compared with women in general), there is still a gap compared with the male teachers. The traditionally low regard for female ability and the social fact of "men surpassing women" have affected the self-esteem of some of the women teachers in higher education. Although the women's liberation movement has undermined traditional concepts, the latter's influence has not been completely eliminated. Although many regarded the social reality of "men surpassing women" in professional achievement as a phenomenon that will gradually change in the course of history, not a few regard it as proof of male superiority. The consequence is that some women teachers in higher education have an overly low evaluation of their own ability, and hence put themselves in a subordinate position both in teaching and in research. We should take note of the fact that low self-esteem is not only found among women teachers with ordinary performance in teaching and research, but even among those with extraordinary research accomplishments, the idea that "woman is inferior to man" still exists. Such low self-esteem results in a lack of self-confidence and competitive spirit that will inhibit the development of their talent. With the introduction of competition in colleges and universities, women teachers have to be bold in competition or they will be eliminated.

The low self-esteem among some of the women teachers in Chinese colleges and universities has led to a gender gap in the perception of professional achievement. As a rule, people with a low self-esteem cannot have a high awareness of professional achievement, but there are other factors as well that affect women teachers in this area. First, when making a choice between their societal and family roles, the scale tips toward "family" rather than "society." In our survey of women faculty and staff members at Beijing University, for instance, 65.8 percent held a negative attitude toward the traditional gender division of work in which "the husband takes care of matters outside the home and the wife takes care of matters inside the home." This reveals that there is still a relatively large proportion of women who hold a positive attitude, or at least not a negative one, inward the concept. To them, it is only right that men are the ones to achieve professionally; they feel that "the husband's success is the wife's success" and sacrifice their own careers for that of their husbands. These women have no other wish as long as they can get by in their work: they have actually voluntarily given up their careers. Second, although some women teachers do want professional achievement, they discover that women have to withstand the pressure and discrimination of the ubiquitous "male cultural standard." They have to go through a lot more trouble to be as successful as males with the same qualifications. Successful women pay a much higher price than successful men. This dampens their wish for success. After getting a clear picture of their unfavorable situation in research and academic competition, they often turn back. They realize they are in an unfair competition where they cannot hope to win even

---

[11] Wei Guoying, "Concise Analysis of Questionnaires Answered by Women Faculty and Staff Members of Beijing University."

after paying an overly high price. The unfairness, to some, is manifested by the following: (1) Unfairness in effective competition time (i.e., women teachers lose a lot of time going through pregnancy, childbirth, and nursing). (2) Unfairness in personal loads. Compared to men, women devote more time to taking care of their families as well as their jobs. (3) Unfairness in opportunities. This mainly refers to such opportunities as on-the-job training, advanced studies, independent handling of topics, selection, and in college and university administration.[12] Women teachers, whose "scales" of life are tipped to ward the family, may have fallen under the influence of the traditional concept of "men take care of matters outside the home, women take care of matters inside the home" and are unwilling to actively participate in career competition. So even though they may not have a low estimate of their abilities, their consciousness of obtaining professional achievement may not be strong.

Since these women teachers do not have strong career aspirations, they would often find excuses to give up their goals, consequently not attaining high career achievement.

In this area, there is a gender difference between men and women. Although it cannot be denied that a certain segment of the women teachers can accurately assess their own abilities, have a strong consciousness of professional achievement, and eventually obtain notable results, this group does not make up a big proportion of women teachers. Among male teachers, the situation is different. Whether from the perspective of the social concept of "men take care of matters outside the home, women take care of matters inside the home" or from family members' expectations, the majority are determined to gain career success. In the colleges and universities, we can see that as a whole women teachers are not as determined and diligent in pursuing higher rank and positions as men. The self-esteem of male teachers is also higher. They may not deny the success of women teachers and may be willing to consider the latter their colleagues, but most would not consider themselves less capable than the women teachers. Few would have a low self-esteem.

Social Identity of Women Teachers in Higher Education

The social identity of women teachers in higher education mainly involves their understanding and evaluation of their role and function as a social group. Here, we will primarily look at their social and family roles, and focus on a comparison with male teachers.

Before reform and the open policy, Chinese society expected women teachers to make accomplishments in society. After reform and the open policy, this social expectation changed to include the dual function of social and family roles. At the same time, with competition gradually introduced in higher educational institutions, the social pressures weighing on women teachers are much heavier than before. Since they are teachers in higher education, they have to keep up with male teachers in making progress and in competition, making professional achievement the value of their existence and the meaning of their lives. With most women teachers having low rank and position, the difficulties they face are much bigger than those of the males. They would have to meet the same criteria as male teachers if they were to change the prejudice against them. At the same time, society is reinforcing their family roles and allows them to devote themselves to their societal role only after they

---

[12] Wang Hongxiong, "Analysis of Competition among Women Intellectuals of Wuhan's Higher Educational Institutions."

perform their family role, or they would be subjected to enormous pressure from public opinion and from their conscience. "A successful professional + good wife and mother" is the societal interpretation of the dual role of women teachers. This concept has penetrated the minds of the public, including the women teachers, thus restricting the latter's choice of their role. A general trend found through surveys in recent years is that women teachers most choose the dual role (career and family) for themselves in regard to gender role; few chose either the family or the career. In the Beijing University survey, for instance, 69.8 percent of the respondents answered that they did not want to neglect either their careers or their families; that they wanted to be both outstanding "career women" and "a good wife and mother"; and 64.6 percent indicated that their greatest happiness was a successful career and a harmonious home. Of the six choices listed under "two things you invested most in your daily life," 69.5 percent picked "teaching, research or other work" and 73.1 percent picked "housework, educating children." This too shows their pursuit of a dual role. For women teachers in higher education, however, to be able to perform both roles well means that they have to withstand a great deal of pressure, causing some of them to work overload and thus reducing the energy and time they could have devoted to their careers. This will affect the future of their careers. These factors gradually whittle away some women teachers' consciousness of career achievement and they focus on their family. This is a most worrisome and sad development. The choice of their role may be considered individual behavior, but in this case, its effect is not limited to themselves. It not only restricts their development, but also provides further ammunition for people who already discriminate against them.

At present, women teachers already make up a fairly large proportion of the total number of teachers in higher education. The public has basically accepted their gradual increase, but there is still a problem in the way they understand and evaluate women teachers as a social group. The general tendency in the evaluation of their teaching and research in recent years has been to affirm their teaching work, but to consider them much behind the male teachers in research findings. It needs to be pointed out that it is a fact that the number of women teachers' research achievements is smaller than the males. Scholars have reached this conclusion by looking at the number of research findings of women teachers in relation to the total number of women teachers, and compared that to men's. Because the number of women teachers is high, the proportion of those with findings is necessarily small. The gender gap in research findings would not be so great if one were to take into account the large numbers of women joining the ranks of teachers in higher education in recent years and the low rank and position of the majority of these women. The gender difference is much smaller among teachers with senior rank and position. Thus, we can foresee that with more women teachers getting higher rank and office, the gender gap in research findings will close.

Society has a low evaluation of women teachers: their intelligence is lower than that of male teachers, they have less ability, and they are not suitable to work in certain disciplines. These views are not hidden in the minds of people but are conspicuously obvious in some so-called research reports. The survey carried out among liberal arts teachers in the science and engineering college mentioned earlier, for instance, obviously reflect these gender prejudices. The researchers of that survey felt that the liberal arts women teachers are weaker than males in intelligence but may be stronger in some nonintelligence factors. According to them, the women teachers had a "reproductive" type of intelligence (good at learning new things) but lacked the developmental and creative types of intelligence (to develop research and pioneer new fields). In temperament, they described women as being narrow-minded, vain, prone to getting overly involved in personal disputes and trivia, while describing men as being strong, determined, self-confident, and open. Although those researchers have not used derogatory words against women, these assessments fully expose their gender prejudices. However, the researchers attributed some problems in higher educational institutions, such as cramming and restricting the scope of tests, to women teachers.[13] One does not know when these issues became women's "exclusive preserve." In fact, these researchers had made women teachers the scapegoat of problems in higher educational institutions today. Although the gender prejudice is veiled among some of them, their estimation of women teachers was still low. They actually represent the views of a segment of society.

The low evaluation of women teachers' ability in society, as "verified" by their low positions, has had the affect of making women teachers believe that "women are inferior to men," or at least that aside from a few particularly brilliant women teachers (they cannot deny the existence of these), most women teachers in higher education are inferior to male teachers. Regrettably, this view has caused some women teachers to lower their own career goals, which only reinforced the belief in their low abilities, thus forming a vicious cycle.

The low estimation of the ability of women teachers not only exists in society, but also in higher educational institutions. This is reflected in the prejudice of researchers, the majority of whom are staff members of such institutions. They therefore represent the views of a portion of the people in higher educational institutions.

The social perception of men is very different. Both society and higher educational institutions hope that male teachers would realize their social roles. After competition was introduced into higher education, the increasingly sharp research and academic competition demanded more time and energy from academics. Whoever put in more time and energy had a higher chance of success. The fact that the expectation of the role of male teachers is relatively unitary puts them, to some extent, in a favorable situation. In addition, the high evaluation society has of male teachers helps them to enter into teaching in higher educational institutions (if they want to), to get promotions in rank and office, and to have higher career goals.

From the above, it can be seen that although the status of women teachers in China's higher educational institutions has risen, the change is not satisfactory. The gap compared with their male counterparts is still rather large. There are many factors, including those inside and outside the higher educational system, that limit a women teacher's status. At the same time, the gap is related to inadequate effort and striving among a part of the women teachers themselves. Hence, we see that improvement of their status is still a ongoing process and needs effort from both the Chinese government and higher educational institutions and from the women teachers themselves.

---

[13] Liu Xiaoming et al., "Exploration of the Feminization of Liberal Arts Teachers in Institutes of Higher Learning."

In: Chinese Women and the Teaching Profession
Editors: Julia Kwong and Ma Wanhua

ISBN 978-1-59033-916-9
© 2009 Nova Science Publishers, Inc.

Chapter 3

THE STATUS AND FUNCTION OF WOMEN TEACHERS IN HIGHER EDUCATION[*]

Pan Houjie

ABSTRACT

The role played by women in different fields has become an important yardstick of social progress and civilization. This article utilizes a survey of women teachers and technicians in Sichuan Province's higher educational institutions to illustrate their rising status and their active role in developing science and technology in the province. The author also makes several suggestions to improve the position of women teachers and technicians.

The world today is paying more attention to the education of women, especially to their higher education. Consequently, the career choices and work of modern women have improved. One of the manifestations of this is the gradually expanding number of women teachers in higher educational institutions (including women doing all types of specialized technical work in these institutions).[†] Since the founding of the People's Republic of China (PRC), the government has paid great attention to the status and function of women in the various fields of the country's modernization. Relatively large strides have been taken in wiping out illiteracy among women and giving them basic, secondary, and vocational education. On this basis, significant progress has been made in providing higher and graduate education to women. All this has laid the foundations for raising women's status and role in the field of higher education. According to statistics, in 1950 (during the first years of the founding of the PRC), there were 17,300 teachers in regular colleges and universities in the

---

[*] Translation © 2000 M.E. Sharpe, Inc., from the Chinese text. Pan Houjie, "Nujiaoshi zai gaodeng jiaoyuzhongde diwei he zuoyong," *Sichuan shifandaxue xuebao (shihui kexue ban)* (Journal of Sichuan Normal University [Philosophy and Social Sciences section]), vol. 23, no. 4, October 1996.

[†] Unless otherwise specified, "women teachers and technical specialists" in this article are used in this context.— Ed.

country, of which only 1,900, or 10.98 percent of the total, were women.[1] By 1994, this number had grown to 396,400,[2] of which 127,000, or 32.1 percent of the total, were women[3]—66.8 times the number in 1950. They have played an appropriate role in the development of higher education and in fostering different types of professional talent. In order to further raise their status in colleges and universities and enable them in play a fuller role, this article shall focus on women teachers and technical professionals in higher education in Sichuan Province and explore the issue.

RISING STATUS AND FUNCTION OF WOMEN TEACHERS AND TECHNICAL SPECIALISTS IN SICHUAN PROVINCE'S HIGHER EDUCATION

According to statistics, on the eve of the founding of the PRC (early 1949), there were only 1,778 teachers of both genders (no data available on women teachers) in the public and private institutions of higher learning in Sichuan Province as a whole.[4] After the founding of PRC, governments at all levels paid great attention and devoted much effort to this issue. By 1994 the number of full-time teachers in the province increased to 25,410, or 14.3 times the 1949 figure. Among them, 7,884 were women, making up 31.03 percent of the total. As far as professional titles and positions are concerned, women made up 15.63 percent of the professors, 24.08 percent of the associate professors, 32.84 percent of the lecturers, 40.09 percent of the assistant professors, and 36.41 percent of the instructors.[5] From the point of view of academic credentials, the proportion of women teachers and technical specialists with graduate credentials and degrees has also risen gradually with the restoration of academic degrees in 1982. According to relevant statistics, by the end of 1994, the percentages of women teachers holding a Ph.D., master's degree, or postgraduate study diploma were, respectively, 10 percent, 24.4 percent, and 23.1 percent. In Sichuan Province, since the mid-1980s most regular undergraduate colleges and universities require the young teachers they hire to have a Ph.D. In 1983 the Sichuan Higher Education Bureau proposed, from a strategical perspective, that all colleges and universities should strengthen their work in raising the levels of young and middle-aged teachers, and especially those who came in after 1981. The Bureau asked all educational institutions to draw up plans and create opportunities in light of teaching and research requirements to enable all young teachers to reach the master's postgraduate level in approximately five years.[6] Colleges and universities have responded by drawing up relevant plans and measures. According to statistics obtained through a survey, in 1994 there were 50,500 technical personnel (including teaching staff and

---

[1] Zhonggno jiaoyu chengjiu, 1949-1983 (Achievements in China's education) (Renmin jiaoyu chubanshe, 1984), p. 102.

[2] Zhonggno jiaoyu bao (China education daily), October 2, 1994, p. 1.

[3] Guangming ribao (Guangming daily), September 6,1995, p. 1.

[4] Zhongguo jiaoyu nianjian 1949-81 (Annals of China's education) (Zhongguo da baike quanshu chubanshe, 1981), pp. 979-80.

[5] Sichuan Tongji Nianjian (Statistical yearbook of Sichuan) (Sichuan tongji ju).

[6] Sichuan sheng gaodeng jiaoyu, zhongdeng zhuanye jiaoyu nianjian, 1949-1985 (Annals of Sichuan higher education and specialized middle school education) (Sichuan jiaoyu chubanshe).

technical specialists) working in the colleges and universities of the province in the scientific, engineering, agricultural, and medical disciplines.[7] Of this number, 20,338 were women, or 40.2 percent of the total. They have instructed and fostered an enormous number of higher-level undergraduates as well as postgraduates who have obtained master's and doctoral degrees, and who have become a major force in the development of science and technology in the province.

In 1994 the province's higher educational institutions engaged in 6,739 scientific research projects of all types, of which 1,026 or 15 percent were on basic topics; 3,377 or 50 percent were in applied fields; and 2,336 or 35 percent were in theoretical fields. They also undertook 523 national science foundation projects, 269 projects are listed as priorities in the eighth five-year plan, and another 886 projects in technical dissemination and service provision. After ten years of effort, they have built 6 priority laboratories and a number of other specialized labs in the country.[8] In all the scientific-technological research projects mentioned above, the rise in the status of women technical specialists and the contributions they have made are clearly evident. For instance, one of the six national-level priority laboratories was established under the leadership of a woman professor of the industrial chemical department at Sichuan United University.

With respect to scientific-technological results, between 1985 and 1994 higher educational institutions in the province won four national science progress awards, twenty-seven national invention awards, and ninety-six national scientific and technological progress awards.[9] The project "new procedure for making ammonium phosphate by concentrating neutralized pulp liquid," invented by a woman professor at Sichuan United University, won first prize at the 1988 national science and technology competition, and was introduced to the whole country. Now, eighty-seven sets of production units have been built, bringing an annual economic benefit of 330 million yuan and raise grain yields by eight million tons. The invention is of major importance to China's chemical fertilizer industry and agricultural output.

The EP—2 ... C4 color film series developer, which was judged to be advanced by world standards, won first prize in Sichuan Province's science and technology competition. It was invented by a women researcher together with another researcher in the chemistry department at Sichuan Teachers University. It is now sold inside the country as well as in some Southeast Asian countries, and is getting good returns. The two inventors put aside a part of their individual income on this product to set up a scholarship fund for graduate and undergraduate students of good scholastic standing and personal character.

In medical and pharmacological research, the proportion of women researchers heading the development of products that have won national and provincial-level awards is also quite impressive. Of these, a Chinese medicinal kidney injection and suppository invented by a group headed by a woman professor of Chinese Medical University was judged to be state-off-the-art by world standards and won first prize at the 1992 National Chinese Medical and Pharmacological Research Competition.

---

[7] Jiaoyu daobao (Education Report), August 22,1995.

[8] Ibid.

[9] Ibid.

The above illustrates the outstanding contributions made by women technical specialists and professors in higher educational institutions in "developing the province through science and education" and in fostering specialized talent.

Statistics show that at the end of 1994 there were 13,170 people engaged in social sciences teaching and research in the higher educational institutions of Sichuan, of which 5,665, or 43 percent of the total, were women.[100] In 1994 they worked on 1,085 different projects in the social sciences, of which 84, or 70 percent of the total, were national social sciences foundation projects. They also published 762 academic works and 4,403 theses, winning 243 social sciences awards at and above the prefectural and municipal levels. Of these 123, or about 48 percent of the total, were issued by provincial authorities or ministries.[111] All of this shows that women are a major force province-wide in social science research.

In addition, in a survey carried out by this author among women teachers and technical specialists at ten institutions of higher learning in the province about their status in assuming leadership positions at various levels, we found that around 30 percent were administrators in teaching research offices or sections; 10 percent were administrators at the department or institute levels; and some were leaders at the college or university level.

This author also found that among the trustees and executives of the Higher Education Research Society of Sichuan, 10.2 percent are women specialists and 14.5 percent are women scholars. They all play an active role in leading scientific research and academic group activities and in decision-making.

As a result of their contributions in teaching and research in the province's universities, many women teachers and technical specialists have won the title of "advanced workers" at different levels. According to statistics published in *Zhongguo jiaoyu bao* (China Education News, May 1, 1995), 59 of the 187 advanced workers in the nation's educational system were from higher educational institutions. Of these, 8 were women, making up 13.6 percent of the total. Of the 10 advanced workers that came from Sichuan, 3 were from higher educational institutions, and one was a woman. Of the advanced teachers and educational workers in the province from 1993-95, 35 worked at institutions of higher learning and 6 were women, making up 17.14 percent of the total.

Despite the above-mentioned progress, the status and function of women teachers and technical specialists in Sichuan still lag behind those in the southeastern coastal regions with advanced cultural development, and in the developed countries. But compared with the situation on the eve of the founding of the PRC, when Sichuan had only a few women teachers among a total of 1,778 teachers in institutes of higher learning, the progress and achievement have been significant.

---

[10] Ibid.

[11] Ibid.

SOME REFLECTIONS ON NEEDED IMPROVEMENTS IN THE SITUATION OF WOMEN TEACHERS AND TECHNICAL SPECIALISTS IN THE PROVINCE'S HIGHER EDUCATIONAL INSTITUTIONS

While we recognize the achievements and progress mentioned above, we should also see that compared with males the status and function of women teachers and technical specialists need to be improved.

First, in the distribution of disciplines, the proportion of women in science, engineering, and high-tech needs to be increased; large numbers of I special measures should be taken to enable women to receive the different levels of basic and higher education.

According to statistics gathered by this author, women made up 43 percent of the 13,200 social science teaching and research personnel in colleges and universities in the province in 1994; they made up, respectively, 26.1 percent, 31.7 percent, 32.3 percent, and 60.8 percent of the 50,500 scientific and technical personnel in the sciences, engineering, agriculture, and medicine. From this it can be seen that in the engineering and technical areas and in the natural sciences, the women's proportion was low as compared to the men's. In another survey made by this author at the end of 1995, full-time women teachers made up 28.6 percent, 31 percent, 32.4 percent, 42.7 percent, and 49.2 percent, respectively, of full-time teachers in four engineering colleges, two agricultural colleges, four teachers colleges, five medical schools, and one foreign language institute in Sichuan: revealing again a relatively low percentage of women teachers in science and engineering colleges. This demonstrates that women are still concentrated in studying and working in traditional specialties like teaching, medicine, and language. An analysis finds that this was mainly caused by obstacles girls encountered in natural science education at the basic level, resulting in low enrollment and graduation in postgraduate studies, especially in the new high-technology specialties in science and engineering colleges and universities. At the same time, an additional factor is the influence of popular traditional concepts of the "women's role," reflected in such sayings as "men take care of matters outside the home while women take care of matters inside the home" and "men are superior and women are inferior," which assign women a supporting role. This has prevented the public's correct appreciation of the significance of women studying natural sciences and production technology, and especially in the study, research, and development of new and high technology. Moreover, this can be examined from the upbringing of girls. We must first admit that urban and rural children of either gender are no different in their natural ability to accept education. However, traditional concepts in Chinese society regard girls as naturally less active than boys, the activity of girls from childhood is much more restricted by parents and society. They thus grow to be quieter, more obedient, and dependent; they have fewer opportunities to train their independence; and their thirst for knowledge and creativity are hampered to some degree. As they grow up—and especially when they go to secondary school—in comparison with the active, mischievous, curious, and gregarious boys, the gap between the two in terms of the breadth and width of their spatial imagination, abstract thinking, and actual hands-on ability becomes more and more obvious. They have misgivings and lack confidence in learning natural sciences such as mathematics and physics. Furthermore, the gap in the evaluation of male arid female cognition and education on the part of some people in society and a few teachers leads them to believe that girls' learning ability is adequate for elementary and junior high schools, but lags behind male students at the senior high level. This makes them neglect the fostering of girls in the learning of such disciplines as math. Parents' and some teachers' unintentional or intentional repression and unbalanced education of girls affects the girls self concept, making them more likely to choose liberal arts when the channeling of arts and science majors occurs in the first year of senior high school. Of course, many girls like liberal arts and choose them, and this is the basis for taking liberal arts or science and engineering college entrance exams. This is another reason for the insufficient numbers of women teachers and technical specialists in today's higher educational institutions.

Under the above circumstances, there are primarily two things that higher educational institutions can do to increase the proportion of women teachers and technical specialists in science, engineering, and new high technology. The first is to strengthen natural science education of girls in basic education. This requires using the media to publicize among parents and society at large, and particularly among rural parents, the idea of "invigorating the nation through science and education." This will help them to fully realize the significance of studying natural sciences and production technology for both boys and girls. Elementary and high schools and educational departments should actively improve objective conditions for boys and girls to receive natural science education and reform teaching content, aids, and methods so as to motivate the girls' enthusiasm for learning the natural sciences. Extra-curricular interest and hobby groups should be organized to encourage and strengthen the girls' self-confidence in science. Science centers for children should be set up to introduce the newest scientific and technological achievements of the world to them, organize scientific popularization programs, and stimulate children's interest in science. The second step is to adopt necessary measures or policies to strengthen women's higher and graduate education. We suggest that, at the input end, science and engineering colleges and new high technology specialties and disciplines with low proportions of female enrollment should give preference to women when other conditions are equal. This is actually not giving girls special preference but counteracting gender prejudice in the admission of new students, thus encouraging women to break through the practice of leaning toward traditional disciplines and choose instead new and high technology majors essential to improving our country's overall strength. They will thus be able to move forward shoulder to shoulder with the males. The fostering of women in undergraduate and graduate education should be given due attention and enhanced to encourage them to excel in their studies. Institutes of higher learning should make every effort to train talented women of highest qualifications in liberal arts, sciences, and engineering who are able to make large contributions to society in an attempt to gradually eliminate prejudices against women in traditional culture. At the output end, colleges and universities should seriously send outstanding women graduates to teach and do research at higher educational institutions.

A second step to further improve the status and function of women teachers is to create objective conditions to raise their teaching and research level as well as their qualifications for promotions in rank and office.

According to 1994 statistics, full-time women teachers in Sichuan Province's higher educational institutions made up, respectively, 15.63 percent of the total number of professors, 24.08 percent of associate professors, 32.84 percent of lecturers, 40.09 percent of assistant professors, and 36.41 percent of instructors. From this it can clearly be seen that the higher the rank and office, the lower the proportion of women. This to a certain extent reflects the fact that the gains in their level of mathematics and scientific research and their achievements are perhaps still below the male teachers. Analysis of the reasons finds that, on the one hand, this has to do with their subjective effort. On the other hand, whether they have the same opportunities for advanced studies that helped male teachers to constantly improve their professional levels, and the opportunities to participate in major research projects to train their abilities, also played a role.

Therefore, objective conditions to raise women's teaching and research levels should be created to improve their qualifications for promotion to higher rank and office and to make greater contributions in work. Higher educational institutions, on the basis of their existing teacher training plans and accomplishments, should continue to improve on-the-job training for women teachers and technical specialists. They should solidly implement the article in the "Education Law of the People's Republic of China" promulgated in 1995, which says: "Schools and related departments should, in compliance with state regulations, ensure women the same rights as men in entering school, advancing to higher studies, employment, receiving academic degrees, and being sent to study abroad." They should organize groups of young and middle-age women teachers, and in particular technical specialists, to receive on-the-job full- or part-time advanced studies at different times. Active efforts should be made to create favorable environments for them to develop and/or participate in major research projects so that they can constantly improve their performance and ability in the practical work of mathematics and research.

Third, effective measures should be taken to continue to train and select women for leading work at all levels in academic organizations so that they inn play a full role in leadership and decision-making.

From a survey of ten Sichuan colleges and universities made by this author, the proportion of women in leadership roles is low compared with male teachers; and the higher the position, the smaller the proportion of women. (Women teachers and technical specialists made up about 30 percent of the heads of teaching research offices and sections; the proportion is around 10 percent for department and institute heads.) In addition, judging from this author's investigation of the situation of women in the Sichuan Higher Education Society, although the executive deputy chairman of the Board of Trustees is a very capable woman researcher, the proportion of women among trustees and executives is still relatively low (10.2 percent and 14.5 percent, respectively). The reason has to do, on the one hand, with subjective factors such as the leadership and organizational ability of the women concerned; on the other, it also has to do with objective factors such as a lack of training of their leadership ability and opportunities to lead. For instance, many people believe that women are patient, detail oriented, earnest, etc. Though well intentioned, such an assessment leads to a closed model or type of personnel management with many women teachers excluded from leadership and decision-making in teaching and research aside from completing their own leaching and research responsibilities. Many women technical specialists are assigned to stay in their offices to do filing, gathering statistics, or campus management. To put it nicely, it is letting women do work which conforms to their characteristics. But under the circumstances, women teachers and technical specialists are not given the opportunity to participate in leadership, or to train and raise their ability to make decisions and do organizational work, which means if they have abilities, they are not using them. Thus there is an appreciable gender gap in the recommendation and selection of leaders.

To improve the situation, the following measures are recommended: First, higher educational institutions should gradually create a cultural atmosphere in which men and women enjoy equal opportunities and women's status is genuinely raised. Besides their own work in the unit, women should be given equal work opportunities to men to enable them to use their leadership talent and train their organizational and decision-making abilities and pioneering and entrepreneurial spirit. This will raise their status and allow them a fuller role in making decisions on major matters in their unit's work. Second, in the current period of social transformation in China (from planned economy to socialist market economy), the practice of having quotas for women in leadership positions at all levels should be combined with open competition and selection of the fittest. After the founding of the PRC, the constitution provided that "women shall enjoy the same rights as men in the political, economic, cultural, and social areas and in family life." People's consciousness, however, often lags behind law, and the traditional concept that "men are the principals and women the accessories" is deeply ingrained among a portion of the population. Moreover, the feudal patriarchal system had lasted for over 2000 years in China under which women were particularly heavily oppressed. After the establishment of the new China, the government made effective efforts to help women participate in national and social development, gaining outstanding results that caught worldwide attention. The State Council, in order to better realize gender equality and enable women to participate in national and social development, issued the "Outline for the Development of Women in China" in 1995. The principal goals during 1995—2000 included " raising women's participation in deciding and managing national and social affairs." On policy and measures, it pointed out: "Substantial efforts shall be made in the fostering and selection of women cadres. Plans should be made to this effect and regularly examined, and should be implemented at each stage"; and "Education and training of women cadres should be reinforced so as to improve their ability to participate in the political process and leadership level." Hence, under present circumstances when social prejudices that discriminate against women still exist, if we abolish the gender ratio and base the leadership selection process purely on competition, women will lose out in selections without gender distinction, thus eliminating some women with true leadership talent. Hence, setting up a quota for women in leadership is most necessary. This practice is not to give preference to women or to demonstrate that women are the weaker sex, but to counteract gender prejudice so that capable leading talent will not be discriminated against and disqualified because of their gender.

Fourth, women teachers and technical specialists should strive to improve their qualities to answer the challenges of the new century.

Lin Lanying, member of the Chinese Academy of Sciences, outstanding woman scientist, and a pioneer of semiconductor research in China, said it well: "To gain equality, one must first rely on one's own efforts." The 1995 State Council "Outline of Women's Development in China" also emphasized: "The broad masses of women must display the spirit of self-respect, self-confidence, self-reliance and self-improvement and seek to make progress and develop in the course of promoting social development." Only self-respect can enable them to profoundly recognize their own worth. Only self-confidence can make them fearless in the face of difficulties and hardships. Only self-reliance can give them independent personalities. Only self-improvement can eventually bring them success. This "four selfs" spirit encourages women to persevere in the truth and climb the heights of their ideals. At present, these "four selfs" have already become powerful ideological weapons in the hands of the masses of women as they move forward to realize their own worth and ideals. Today in particular, at the crossroads of two centuries, when a new situation has arisen in China's reform, opening, and modernization, and when we face fierce global economic, cultural, scientific, and technical competition, the quality of women affects the quality of the nation. The development level of women affects a country's overall strength. Women teachers and technical specialists of higher educational institutions should further intensify their self-respect, self-confidence, self-reliance, and self-improvement, overcome their weaknesses, ceaselessly improve their quality and sense of competition, and seek progress and improvement in promoting social development. They should strive to make greater contributions to the development of higher education in China, in fostering talented people of all types into the next century, and in realizing the goals of the ninth five-year plan and of 2010.

PART II: FEMINIZATION OF TEACHING

In: Chinese Women and the Teaching Profession
Editors: Julia Kwong and Ma Wanhua

ISBN 978-1-59033-916-9
© 2009 Nova Science Publishers, Inc.

Chapter 4

INITIAL EXPLORATION OF THE PHENOMENON OF THE FEMINIZATION OF TEACHERS[*]

Fu Songtao

The Department of Education at Hebei University, Hebei,China

The feminization of teachers as a social group is a change that has occurred in the gender structure of Chinese teachers in the past dozen years or so. Its significant impact on the overall quality of China's teaching resource and the effective practice of educating and teaching is becoming increasingly obvious. At a deeper level, it reflects the inertia of the traditional culture and objective changes in Chinese society. This phenomenon needs to be studied from both the theoretical and applied perspectives.

Feminization of teachers refers to the fact that the female to male ratio in the group (greater than 1.5:1) is significantly higher than the normal gender ratio (around 1:1) in society, and that the individual character and behavior of members of the group have acquired clearly softer characteristics. Data shows that feminization has become a major feature of China's teaching profession, especially at the elementary and secondary school levels in large and medium-sized urban communities. What is even more worth noting is that the individual character and behavior of teachers are becoming softer and weaker. Members of the group have generally demonstrated such feminine traits as softness, gentleness, serenity, sensitivity, conservatism, prudence, timidity, and weakness in their individual character. They overly pursue the feminine moral culture; they are too tolerant, conciliatory, restrained, and indulgent toward students. Members of these teachers as a social group tend to favor, guide, and affirm students whose orientations and behavior show obedience, meekness, and conformity; they are often cold or give negative evaluations to students who are rugged and spirited, frank and open, and independent with a strong character. They are prone to use feminine education methods such as persuasion, guidance, giving hints and insinuations, and trying to move students emotionally. They are afraid to use restraining and controlling

---

[*] Translation © 2000 M.E. Sharpe, Inc., from the Chinese text. Fu Songtao, "Jiaoshi qunti nuxinghua xianxiang chutan," *Jiaoyu pinglun* (Education Commentary), no. 5, 1997.

methods such as dissuasion, prohibition, criticism, or warning to set strict demands on students and show their genuine concern.

The feminization of teachers has obvious negative effects on the healthy development of the students' character and even personality, and hence on the competitive type of talented people modern society needs. Whether from the perspective of individual members of society or of society as a whole, a healthy character and personality should be well balanced—both strong and soft. It should possess the women's gentleness, serenity, docility, patience, generosity, and love; along with the strength, boldness, ruggedness, independence, self-confidence, and dignity of men. At a critical time when youngsters, especially elementary school students, are forming a healthy individual character and personality, a prolonged period of exposure to the subliminal and constant influence of a feminized teacher group and education make it hard for male vigor and energy to be born, nurtured, and grow among the students; while feminine softness, on the other hand, is implanted and grows. Intentionally or unintentionally, this will make the students strongly affected by "rouge and powder" femininity and fail to achieve the necessary balance in strength and softness. Observant people have noticed that not only do girl students take particular care with their appearance, putting on makeup and talking in a small, delicate voice, acting in an indecisive and unrevealing way, but some boy students, too, act the same way, and sometimes even go further. We can foresee that our new members of society may have an excess of yin-softness and inadequate yang-vigor. They lack the masculine traits of daring to blaze new trails, strength, courage, boldness, and forthrightness at a time when reform and opening is surging forward, the pace of life is speeding up, and competition has become increasingly acute. A feminized personality is glaringly out of step with the social atmosphere.

The feminization of the teacher group has, to a certain extent, weakened the internal competition and cooperation among members of society, thus depleting it of necessary life and vitality and making it hard for members to maximize their effort in cooperation. Compared with men, women possess a weaker sense of competition, are slower to take part, and less intense in competition. Under the influence of the traditional family concept in China and the specific role assigned to women, and because of the effect of the feminine way, women compete mostly in a hidden and irregular way, and the goal and means of competition are often unprofessional. In particular, after they marry and have children, they undertake most of the housework and building a family occupies an increasingly important place in their hearts. Their feeling of satisfaction is often centered in the home. All this results in a lack of open and professional competition among members of the teacher group. Moreover, because of the individual nature of teaching, they often neglect and even ignore necessary cooperation, sometimes even resorting to unethical means of competition to go after each other. Thus, the group's viability and coherence is sharply hurt.

The feminization of the teacher group is also one of the major underlying causes of its low social status. Patriarchy is a relatively common phenomena of human culture. People generally evaluate highly the social status of male occupations, thus raising the social status of groups engaging in those occupations. Chinese society is deeply influenced by traditional feudal culture and the concept of "male superiority and female inferiority" is deeply entrenched in the minds of many citizens. Subconsciously, they look down the ways of life and habits of women, and particularly women's occupations. People have a misunderstanding of the individual and social value of education and a bias toward and low regard for the requirements and specialization in the teaching profession. They view the results of education as uncertain and not practical. All these lead to the weakness, low participation, and the nonmaterial nature of the feminized teaching profession. It is therefore inevitable that the social status of the feminized teacher group and the teaching profession should be so low in the minds of people.

The causes of the feminization of the teacher group are varied. Many factors are interrelated and move in a vicious cycle. For instance, the traditional concept of "male superiority and female inferiority" in the subconscious of people leads to the negative evaluation of the social status of the teaching profession to which many women belong. Social opinion, in turn, leads competitive males to be unwilling to join, or to leave, the teaching profession, leaving a fair number of vacancies to be filled by more women. The increase of women further weakens the competitiveness of the teacher group and lowers its social status, with the result that even fewer males, who are highly competitive in nature, are willing to go into that profession. Members of society who seek stability and women flow into teaching in greater numbers, thus enhancing the feminization of the group.

The feminization of the teacher group is objectively inevitable. The traditional concept of education, social organization, and the renaissance of the yin-softness culture after reform and opening made this inevitable and developed to the extreme. From a comparative perspective, in the United States and the former Soviet Union, women make up over 70 percent of elementary and secondary school teachers. The feminization of teachers has become one of the important factors triggering violence in U.S. elementary and secondary schools. The delayed effect of education, the subjectivism of the targets of education, the ambiguity of educational labor and standards, and the nonmaterial nature of educational work all make it hard for educational activity, like material productive activity, to have clear qualitative and quantitative targets, standardized operation procedures, strict measures and criteria for awards and penalties, and genuine competition. Objectively, this has weakened the competitiveness of teaching and softened teaching labor to make it more feminine. In addition, the long-term and repetitive nature of the educational process and results, and the immaturity of the targets of education demand sustained stamina, patience, rich emotions, and feelings on the part of participants. The female physiological and psychological characteristics doubtlessly and clearly are suitable for this role. Thus, it is advantageous and inevitable that more women are choosing the teaching profession.

However, the above is not enough to feminize the teacher group. It is the distorting effect of the following causes that feminized the role of the teacher group.

The first is the effect of the traditional social organization. A highly centralized social control model and organization require all members of society to play their separate social roles, to obey and conform to their fixed roles, thus forming a widespread yin-softness cultural atmosphere and personality. Teachers as members of society living in this cultural atmosphere will doubtlessly acquire corresponding or similar personalities. More importantly, since education is an instrument and tool for training obedient and conforming talent, feudal ruling classes through the ages had imposed increasingly strict demands to make an example and model of conformity. It further enhanced the conforming and obedient character and consciousness of individuals, imbuing teachers with more feminine characteristics. The traditional Chinese social organization and mode of competition is closed and lacks openness, professionalism, and standardization. The educated society as a major carrier and primary channel of dissemination of traditional culture shares similar structural identity and competitive mode as society as a whole. This is an important factor in educating society to utilize the covert type of competition and further reinforces the feminization of the teacher group.

Second, the one-sided guidance of the neotraditional education theory is another major reason for the feminization of the teacher group. The starting point of neotraditional education theory turns from societal to individual standard, one-sidedly emphasizing the absolute reasonableness of children's interests and ignoring the basic differences between the school environment and real life. It does not see the need for a competitive atmosphere and organization in school or its role in fostering students' competitive awareness and ability. It asks teachers to be "shepherds herding the flock"—to take care of and guide students. Restrictive or strict educational methods are considered violations of children's rights and repression of their individual characters. In addition, our educational theory also starts out from the requirement to build a new type of interpersonal relationship and provides a "soft" and pleasant education to students, overly emphasizing teachers' soft qualities such as patience, kindness, love, generosity, and accommodation.

After reform and opening, the resurgence of the yin-softness culture and the enhancement of competitive social life further stimulated the teacher group to move toward feminization. The Chinese—in the midst of sustained and fierce political and ideological struggle, like people in the West who are in the midst of the whirlpools of economic competition—desperately need to relax their tense nerves stretched to the breaking point. They long to relax their stiff and tired bodies with light music and soft emotions. Thus, the soft and aesthetic culture spearheaded by light music and romantic fiction came in and spread to all realms of society. The education field as the frontlines for the dissemination of culture, considered to have been a left-over from the yang-vigor culture, naturally even more urgently underwent soft-aesthetic transformation, or even feminization. Of course reform and opening have provided the opportunities and sites for even sharper, more open and sustained competition: the education department in comparison appears to be even softer and more feminine.

To have a new understanding of the characteristics of the human resources required by the new economic system and social organization and the changing traditional functions of education is the ideological basis and starting point for changing the feminization of the teacher group. We must see that the talents needed in the fundamentally competitive market economy are people who are competitive, adaptable to change, and creative. They should possess broad and solid knowledge, mature conduct, and good skills. They also have an innovative spirit and the corresponding psychological qualities such as boldness in competition, daring to take risks, capability of withstanding setbacks, undaunted by failures, self-restraint, and discipline. They would not try to get other people's sympathy and pity to get out of their own responsibilities. In short, a society where competition is becoming ever sharper needs its members to have a strong yang-vigor spirit, and the traditional "soft education" and "education as a tool of society" cannot fulfill this onerous historical task. Only competitive education can turn out competitive people and only by training competitive people can education meet the needs of, and keep pace with, the times. The competitive type of education can only be provided by a nonfeminized teacher group with competitive individual character and behavior. Hence, raising the percentage of male teachers to correct the feminization of the teacher group and reinforce the yang-vigor characteristic is the inevitable demand of the socialist market economy.

The fundamental way to change the feminization of teachers is to improve teaching methods to enhance competition in education. Competitive education is manifested in the use of competitive educational methods and the implementation of competitive educational organization. Dissuasion, persuasion, and guidance are effective educational methods, but for them to function, there must be strict rules, regulations, discipline, and appropriate restraints. School education will foster students' competitive consciousness and train their competitive mentality and skills only when it faithfully simulates a competitive environment and mechanism similar to that in real life. For this purpose, the schools must establish an effective system of evaluation and elimination, set high teaching standards, require teachers to rationally and boldly use criticism, dissuasion, prohibition, and even penalties to stimulate, train, and enhance the nonfeminine qualities of the individual character and the behavior of the teacher group.

The gender ratio of the teacher group should be strictly controlled and conditions created for outstanding male members in society to enter the teacher group. Women teachers do not necessarily lead to the feminization of the teacher group, but the phenomenon of their extraordinary growth in numbers is, after all, the major indication, foundation, and cause of the group's feminization. Hence, controlling their extraordinary increase is the most practical preventive measure to change the group's feminization. First, a quota for an appropriate gender ratio should be set. Taking into consideration the specific requirements of the actors in education, the male : female ratio in elementary schools should be 1:1.5; in secondary and higher educational institutions, the ratio should be at the normal rate. In view of the significant lack of male teachers at the present time, and inline with the correct principle of "to each according to his/her work and equal pay for equal work," we should recognize the objective gender difference between male and female, create competitive opportunities and conditions for male teachers, and provide them with greater pay for greater work so that more males may be attracted into the ranks.

In pointing out the current situation of the negative influences and causes of the feminization of teachers and measures for improvement, I have no wish to deny the important status and function of the yin-softness in effective educational activity. Neither do I deny the major contributions made by the broad masses of women teachers to education. Even less do I wish to keep them out of the teacher group. The examination and recommendations made in this article emanated from my misgivings about the negative impact that the feminization of the character and conduct of teachers will have on the outcomes of education and the social status of teachers. I hope this article has provided some useful suggestions to change our educational ideology at a time when the country is transforming into a new economic social system.

REFERENCES

Liu Kangde. *Yinxing wenhua* (Yinxing culture). Shanghai People's Publishing House, April 1994.

Yu Yan. *Nuxing renleixue* (Female anthropology). Oriental Publishing House, June, 1988.

Min Jiayin et al. *Yang-gan yu yin-rou de bianzou* (The variations of yang-vigor and yin-softness). Chinese Social Sciences Publishers, September 1995.

Shan-chuan-li. *Zhongguo nuxingshi* (History of the female sex in China). Translated by Gao Dalun and Fan Yong. San Qin Publishers, July 1987.

Li-sha Si-gang-ci-ni et al. *Jiaose bianqianzhongde nanxing yu nuxing* (Male and female in changing roles). Translated by Pan Jianguo et al. Zhejiang People's Publishing House, August 1988.

In: Chinese Women and the Teaching Profession
Editors: Julia Kwong and Ma Wanhua

ISBN 978-1-59033-916-9
© 2009 Nova Science Publishers, Inc.

Chapter 5

THE FEMINIZATION OF STUDENT BODIES OF NORMAL SCHOOLS AND MEASURES TO COUNTER IT[*]

Shi Jinfang

The Chinese Department at Nantong Specialized Teachers College,
People's Republic of China

At the turn of the century, the most critical issue facing Chinese basic education is how to implement quality education *(suzhi jiaoyu)*. As we put our attention to the quality of teaching in basic education, a notable phenomenon cannot but arouse our attention: In recent years, the majority of students on campuses of normal schools are women. We can project that after the feminization of teachers in kindergartens and elementary schools, a similar trend will appear in junior high schools. This is especially notable in coastal areas where the economy is developed. What influence is this trend going to bring to the quality of teachers as a social group or to the quality of basic education? This has to be considered a new issue in education, in teaching reform in normal schools, and in overall quality education.

INCREASING TREND OF NORMAL SCHOOL STUDENTS BECOMING PREDOMINANTLY FEMALE, AND ITS SOCIAL CAUSES

The gender ratio of admission in the past few years at Nantong Normal College, where this author works, shows that prior to 1987, apart from the English major, admission of female students in every other major was under 35 percent of the total. In mathematics and physics, the percentages were around 10, and for two years were actually 1 percent and 2 percent. From 1988-94, the number of females admitted exceeded 50 percent. In 1993, the figure was over 70 percent in the Chinese major and in 1994 over 80 percent. Similar situations prevailed in other normal schools in Jiangxi Province, and this rate will remain the same for the next few years. This reveals at least two issues: (1) The gender ratio of students

---

[*] Translation © 2000 M.E. Sharpe, Inc., from the Chinese text. Shi Jinfang, "Shizhuan xuesheng nushenghua qushi jiqi duice,"Jiangsu gaojiao(gaojiao guanli), no.6, 1997.

in normal schools has lost its balance and become predominantly female and (2) economic development is affecting young people's career choices.

The feminizing trend of students in such schools has a historical background and deep social causes. This is mainly shown in the following respects.

The Market Economy Has a Strong Impact on Male Values

At present people's ideas, values, and pace of life have all come under the assault of the market economy. This is especially true of young people, who have been quickly dominated by new wishes and desires, including:

A. *The wish to ride the waves.* The surging waves of reform and opening first hit the coastal areas and then swept through the country. Many daring swimmers, unwilling to be left behind, jumped "into the sea" (*xiahai*). Some teachers do not want to spend their youth behind the teaching lectern and want to see the world. Very few young people sign up for the teaching specialty when they submit their applications.

B. *The desire for wealth.* Many men are frustrated to see the lifestyle of people who "got rich first" but have no special talent. It becomes hard for them to maintain their mental equilibrium. When possession of wealth be comes a feeling of male accomplishment, the desire for wealth becomes uncontrollable. Plain and poorly-paid teaching jobs hold no attraction.

C. *The pursuit of pleasure.* With the sharp increase in material consumption, "enjoying life's pleasures" becomes a realistic and fashionable philosophy of life. The formerly admired impoverished and monotonous life of a recluse is ridiculed by modern hedonism. Many male students in normal schools enroll because of a lack of other alternatives. They come because their families are poor, their grades are not good enough to be accepted by other schools, or their homes are in the rural areas and parents need them to have an "iron rice bowl."

In addition, most graduates in recent years have been placed in junior high schools at the village level. The location is remote, school conditions are poor, and the male students do not think they will come to much. Some may even have a hard time even finding a suitable wife. The plummeting number of male students at these schools can better be understood and becomes reasonable when the above factors are taken into account.

Social Transformation is Leading to a Regression of the Female Role

Changes in society gradually make the male role in the commodity economy more important, so women who formerly enjoyed the same financial position as men in the family are gradually returning to the role of the men's "domestic assistants." Thus appeared the phenomenon of women' role regression. Under these general circumstances, the teaching profession has acquired added attraction in the eyes of women because:

A. *It is a secure and dignified profession.* The market economy is filled with brutal competition. Although some strong women have pushed into the midst of the males and succeed, the majority are stressed out and cannot take care of all matters at once. This makes ordinary women yearn for a stable job. Those with some education long even more for a dignified job. Teaching, though a tiring and low-paid job, is respected. Teachers are rarely under other people's control and enjoy relative personal space as well as security, and that is why women prefer the profession.

B. *It gives women favorable conditions to support their husbands and teach their children.* In the public mind, teachers are educated and sensible people. They are learned and possess good moral values, and are adept at using teaching skills. To people busy in their careers, they are ideal candidates for spouses. In a nation like ours centered around the male, the actions of women to a certain degree depend on the likes and dislikes of men. Moreover, with the single child's education and training becoming the foremost priority in every family, a wife that is a teacher is tantamount to having a good private tutor at home. Male preferences for their wives often become the criteria women use to shape their own images.

C. *It enables them to express unique maternal love.* Maternal love is inborn in women. Little girls play mother and also love to play house. These emotions give them a unique love for children and qualify them for being teachers. Becoming teachers also gives them an outlet for their maternal love. From this it can be seen that women identify with teaching and women teachers are inevitable products of social transformation. The gender regression of women comes from the need to combine social life and family work and is also the realistic and sensible choice that women make. The predominantly female enrollment in normal schools is no accident and cannot be controlled in a short period of time. The study and exploration of the effect of this trend on quality education is extremely necessary.

Potential Effects that Must be Faced

Women have a lot of advantages in teaching as compared with men. However, if the gender ratio becomes imbalanced and the teaching field becomes feminized, then quality education will be negatively impacted.

Although human quality is affected by hereditary factors, postnatal education and environment are even more important. The teacher's role and influence on students during the basic education period is pivotal. What negative effects can the feminization of junior high school teachers produce on the shaping and development of students' quality? We can examine this from the following six perspectives.

(1) From the perspective of imagery affects. Every teacher will have some kind of imagery affect on students. The smaller the students, the stronger their imitation of the external image of teachers. For instance, boys or girls in kindergarten act in a feminine when telling stories way mainly because kindergarten teachers are all females. If students have mainly gentle and loving women teachers and experience teaching more like an outpouring of maternal love, they will miss the deeper and tougher male image as a role model. This would

be very detrimental to students whether in molding their personalities and image or in the formation of a healthy psyche.

(2) From the perspective of intellectual structure. Studies reveal that the intelligence of women normally belongs in the middle range. This, together with the effect of many other factors such as tradition, mindset, environment, society, and the family, makes women generally more conservative and closed-minded than men. This is shown in the following characteristics. First, they lack a strong desire to pursue new knowledge, especially cutting-edge information in newly emerging disciplines. During the present information age when there is a knowledge explosion, their intellectual structure appears narrow and outdated, and their range of knowledge relatively narrow. Second, they lack a keen inquisitive mind for new issues. The rapid development of society raises the question of how to adapt to its pace. Although basic education is targeted at unworldly youngsters and teenagers, we still must never ignore society's influence on them. Socialization is a complex social process occurring among these young people and teachers have to be sensitive to societal influences and study the situation seriously so that they can guide students in accordance with the circumstances and teach them what they need in order to foster modern people with a strong adapt ability. Because of the strong influence of their family role and their relatively weaker social consciousness, women teachers find it hard to keep up with society's pace and reveal the weaknesses of being old-fashioned and behind the times. Third, they do not generally have a strong ability to per form experiments. It has been found in the engineering departments of normal schools that female students are generally not as good as male students in conducting experiments. This is demonstrated by their apprehension at actually doing experiments, their strong dependence on other people, and their lack of perspective on different phenomena. As a result, it is hard for them to grasp the internal connection between the essence of things. In doing experiments, it is hard for them to have bold and unique ideas and they lack the innovative and inventive quality in thinking. In short, their weaknesses in intellectual structure limit their development, but as teachers will directly affect the intellectual development of their students. Youth is a critical time for youngsters and teenagers to develop their intellect. These adverse influences would affect them not merely for a short time, but for their whole lives.

(3)From the perspective of emotions and willpower. Women teachers possess rich and delicate sensibilities, which can have a positive effect in education and teaching. The tremendous success gained in affective teaching by the elementary school teacher Li Jilin and the secondary school teacher Yu Yi proves this. But the ruggedness, depth, reserve, and kindliness of male emotions is something that women cannot compare. The special character of these male emotions has a profound influence on the determination and firmness of the students' character. With the decreasing number of male teachers, this influence too is weakening. The social phenomenon that is constantly appearing in recent years is the "feminization of boys." Of course, there are many causes for this, but the feminization of the ranks of teachers is one of them. Not only do the emotions and feeling of teachers influence students in a subliminal way, but teachers must also intentionally foster and temper students' willpower. Here the gender difference is also obvious. When a mother walks with a child, she would always hold the child's hand and repeatedly tell him or her, "Go slowly, don't run!" A father on the other hand would staunchly encourage the child, "Run, run quickly!" Should the child fall, the mother would rush over and pick up the child, while the father would tell the child, "Get up, little man!" This demonstrates how women always want to protect the weak

and put them under their wings, while men would encourage the weak to become stronger on their own. These two different attitudes express two different views of education: Women teachers are always removing obstacles and lessening the challenges for students, while male teachers intentionally set up obstacles and let the students experience setbacks. As a result, the former actually increases the students' dependence and inertia, and the latter tempers students willpower and enables them to better adapt to things.

(4) From the perspective of ideals and aspirations. Guidance is indispensable in the formation of ideals. If in childhood many beautiful dreams and fancies are illusory, then the teenage years are the first critical period when a human being forms his or her ideals and aspirations. Though not yet completely free of childishness, teenagers start to acquire adult ideas and use their intelligence to think over things to make judgments or choices. Teenage years are a time of ardor and stubbornness; once an aspiration or interest is formed, it is not easily discarded, and sometimes lasts through life. However, this period is also a time when kids have exaggerated opinions of their abilities, do things blindly, and may easily go astray. This is a critical period when youths acquire ideals and aspirations, and a dangerous time when they might form unhealthy ideas and interests. Hence correct guidance and positive influence is essential. Secondary school is the crucial time for teenagers; the demand on the quality of the teachers should be higher, but this point has not received enough attention. The serious gender imbalance explains this. Naturally, we are not saying that the quality of women teachers is not good, only that they are generally more conservative, are not strongly motivated to move forward, are emotional and sometimes not rational, do not examine issues too deeply, and do not think much into the future. These are all objective traits. Under a market economy in particular women have a strong propensity to regress in their role. This factor and their heavy burdens in the family weaken their professional ideals and career pursuits. All this will keep them from giving good guidance to students about ideals and aspirations.

(5) From the perspective of individual character. At present, the biggest flaw in examination-oriented education lies in ignoring the development of students' individual character and potential. This precisely proves that the most important mission of quality education is to help students form a fine character and qualities, and to tap their creativity to the full. However, with the feminization of teachers, we have reason to be worried that another difficulty has been added to the existing ones in quality education: that is, most women teachers have the standard that "obedient students are good students" and this attitude causes some students who want to be "good" to suppress their own wishes and learn to be accommodating, docile, observant of what others want of them, and obedient. We should know that when students are obedient to teachers, they are actually suppressing their own character at the cost of their own personalities. If this goes on, they lose their uniqueness and become, like bonsai plants, praiseworthy works of art without individual character. A few stubborn students who act with independence and hence break "disciplines" and "rules" are dubbed "bad students." This marks them for the cold shoulder treatment and hurts their feelings. This seriously harms their chances of acquiring good individual qualities. Actually, people who make great accomplishments are often those who are adventuresome and daring since childhood. The feminization of students' character by teachers will obviously weaken them and make them mediocre, thus depriving them of the critical foundation for fostering fine qualities which build individual character.

(6) From the perspective of the building up of the teaching ranks. The gender ratio imbalance leads male students to the erroneous impression that men do not stoop to become teachers. Thus, the teaching profession is excluded from the list of male career choices. The distorted cycle of examination-oriented education will cause a crisis in the teacher's image, resulting in the profession losing any attraction among students. According to a report in the July 27, 1997, *Workers Daily* (Gongren ribao), a survey of 10,000 elementary school pupils in Beijing found less than 6 percent wanted to grow up to be teachers, workers, or farmers (3.5 percent, 2.2 percent, and 0.2 percent, respectively). This shows that the teaching resource for basic education has fallen into a vicious cycle, and one of the links is feminization. This has brought and will bring serious consequences to quality education.

Today people are actively exploring the theoretical and practical issues of quality education. Quality education is necessary but makes little progress. A major topic facing education reform in normal schools targeted at training junior high school teachers is the measures to be adopted to solve the critical problem of feminization, which has such a serious influence on the teaching structure and quality of teachers.

URGENT REFORM MEASURES

To rectify the imbalance in students' gender ratio in normal schools and to improve the quality of the teaching contingent, the government must adopt genuinely effective measures—including increasing funds for normal schools, giving priority to school facilities and favored treatment to student fees, enacting policies to ensure the number and quality of students, determining a fixed gender ratio in enrollment, and greatly raising teacher salaries and benefits to make the teaching profession truly respected and admired. This way we can hope to form a supportive relationship between teacher recruitment and education quality.

Normal schools whose aim is to train qualified junior high teachers may not be able to change the overall teacher structure, but they can, through education and teaching reform, improve the quality of the predominantly female student body. This is a huge task before us in improving basic quality education; it is also a basic question in improving school quality and education. This author thinks that reform can be concentrated in the following areas.

Turning Specialized Knowledge and Skills Education into Overall Quality Education

Teacher education cannot be considered an ordinary branch of vocational education. Ordinary vocational education trains skilled craftsmen of different types, and all one needs is specialized knowledge and skills. Teacher education does not train people in the craft of teaching, but educators and specialists in nurturing human beings. For a human being to develop and become a talented professional, many factors are involved and the teacher's mission is to help students find and tap favorable factors and to avoid and overcome unfavorable factors, so that each student develops in the most favorable way and realizes his or her most meaningful life's values. This requires teachers to have good qualities, and even more important than excellent professional qualities, sound ideological qualities including correct values on life and the world and dedication to education and pursuit of one's ideals. They should help students return from their regressive role and become forward looking and enterprising.

Turn the Closed Curriculum into an Open Curricular Structure

Since the Normal Education Division of the State Education Commission announced in 1995 the new teaching plan for normal education, relevant schools have adjusted their curriculums, but it remains for the most part closed. Its goal is to pass on specialized knowledge with skills training courses that are fragmented and piecemeal. We must design courses targeted to the concrete situation of the students, such as the fact that there are more girls than boys. The content should be more varied, the courses should include more electives and focused more on training. In short, they should be structured in an open and pluralistic way so as to give students more opportunities to learn to develop and improve their qualities in a systematic way.

Replace a Monastic Impractical Teaching Mode with a Society-oriented Teaching Pattern

At the present time, higher normal colleges and universities are not very different from comprehensive colleges and universities in teaching mode. Their knowledge systems are similar—adhering to the original disciplinary boundaries; their teaching modes are similar— the monastic impractical type of lecturing. There is even a tendency to violate the philosophy of education, namely, competition and emulation. Teacher colleges and universities try to emulate comprehensive universities: specialized schools emulate specialized colleges and lose sight of their own goal in education. For instance, to meet the needs of compulsory education, Jiangsu Province Education Commission wants normal colleges to graduate junior high teachers with college degrees. The colleges, out of a blind wish to emulate comprehensive universities, put their focus on foreign languages or computers; liberal arts departments increase classroom time in higher math and physical science. We do not, of course, want to overlook the use of foreign languages and computers as tools in future society and neither are we against widening students' range of knowledge. We only feel that such teaching reform is not realistic. What kind of teachers does quality education in junior high school need most? In what ways are key teachers of junior high with an undergraduate education better than those with specialized education? Does improvement of foreign language and computer classes translate into the improvement in a teacher's quality? We must not act on assumptions and emulate blindly; we must break through the monastic impractical kind of teaching and develop society-oriented education based on social need. Only by so doing can our schools and teaching reform remain on the correct path and maintain vitality.

(Editor-in-charge: Gu Guanhua)

PART III: BECOMING TALENTED PROFESSIONALS

In: Chinese Women and the Teaching Profession
Editors: Julia Kwong and Ma Wanhua

ISBN 978-1-59033-916-9
© 2009 Nova Science Publishers, Inc.

Chapter 6

INITIAL ANALYSIS OF THE FACTORS ENABLING WOMEN TEACHERS IN HIGHER EDUCATION TO BECOME TALENTED PROFESSIONALS[*]

Zhou Xin

Women make up an integral half of human society, an important, organic part of China's human resources. Taking women college teachers as an example, in 1950 there were only 2,139 throughout the whole country. By 1981, this number had increased 26.9 times to 62,496 (quoted from "Women Psychology," Liaoning University Press). By 1991, the number had increased even faster, to 116,400, or 29.1 percent of the country's total. At the same time, many women teachers have assumed leadership posts in schools. Along with the continuous increase in numbers and the rise in status, women teachers are playing a more important role than any time before. They have become an indispensable force in higher education in China. It is their wish to become truly talented professionals. To aid in this goal, this article shall explore from the perspective of women's psychology the conditions for women teachers to become truly talented professionals in higher education, the obstacles they face, and measures they can take to overcome these obstacles.

CONDITIONS FOR WOMEN TEACHERS TO BECOME TALENTED PROFESSIONALS IN HIGHER EDUCATION

Generally speaking, there are two conditions for women teachers in higher education to become talented professionals: external and internal. External conditions mainly refer to the social atmosphere, school, and home environments. Today, raising women's political status is the prerequisite for women teachers to become talented professionals. The rigor and development of the economy and rising cultural and scientific levels have a major impact on

---

[*] Translation © 2000 M.E. Sharpe, Inc., from the Chinese text. Zhou Xin, "Gaoxiao nujiaoshi chengcai yingshu qianxi," *Guangxi daxue xuebao (zhexue shehuikexue ban)* (Guangxi University Bulletin [Philosophy and Sociology section]), no. 3, 1993.

their becoming talented professionals. In schools, the composition and deployment of talent and the quality of the conditions for teaching and research have a direct impact on the speed and timing of women becoming talented professionals. In family relations, the relations are closest between husband and wife, and the mutual understanding, support, encouragement, and help of the husband and wife are no doubt a powerful support to each in becoming truly talented and have a direct effect on the wife's talent and development. Internal conditions include physiological and psychological conditions and constitute the physical and mental foundations for women to become talented professionals. Women have stronger resistance against diseases than men, and this is to their advantage, giving them favorable conditions for becoming talented professionals. As far as mental factors are concerned, these can be divided into intellectual and nonintellectual factors.

What are the Merits of the Female Intellect?

First, from the cognitive perspective, women have stronger reading ability and have greater concentration. They have good memories. In teaching and research, these qualities enable them to concentrate and increase the efficiency of their observation, memory, imagination, and thinking. They feel that the key to their becoming talented professionals lies in the correspondence between their concentration and the demands of their educational occupation. They are therefore able to constantly increase their knowledge, adjust their interests, and increase the time and energy to develop their abilities so that they can become useful talented professionals in higher educational institutions.

Second, in terms of mode of thinking, women are good at thinking in images and fluent in expression. This is very useful to them as teachers giving lectures in classrooms. They speak clearly, enunciate words distinctly, have a gentle tone, and can liven up the classroom. In order to get better teaching results, they closely observe the changes on the face of each student in class to get immediate feedback, find out how well the students are absorbing their lessons, analyze, and employ flexible teaching methods at any time.

Third, women have strong powers of observation and are capable in uncovering problems. They are able to observe minute details often overlooked by men and discover problems. This is very useful to teaching and research in higher education.

Nonintellectual factors mainly refer to emotions, willpower, and personality. From ancient times to today, many famous women specialists and educators in China and other countries possess—besides high intellectual ability – warm emotions, a persistent willpower, and an independent character. it is hard to image anyone who lacks willpower and is afraid of committing him or herself making great accomplishments in his or her work.

Obstacles in the Way of Women Teachers Becoming Talented Professionals

The impediment to women teachers becoming talented professionals in higher education comes first of all from society. The pernicious influence of erroneous traditional viewpoints carried down from feudal society remains to this day. Even when men and women are equal in economic status, the progress of history has not completely changed some men's traditional demands on women. They explicitly demand women to be "obedient" and "docile," and if women persist in their own ideas and stubbornly pursue career success, they accuse them of being "not womanlike." Should a certain woman become a conspicuous talent, some people would be very alarmed. Society's low expectation of women adds to the obstacles women face in becoming talented professionals. People expect men to have greater accomplishments in all fields, and praise and admire such men. They have no such expectations toward women: this fully shows their low expectations. The same situation prevails in regard to women teachers in higher education becoming talented professionals.

Second, obstacles to women teachers becoming talented professionals also come from the family. For physiological reasons, women have many specific interests and demands different from men's. Like men, they have to he creators of material and intellectual wealth, but they also shoulder the special mission of propagating the human race. Hence, traditional concepts cause many women to spend a great deal of time and energy on caring for children and the home. One survey shows that among young and middle-aged female intellectuals about 70 percent spend over 3 hours in housework every day. Burdensome work at home takes away their time for study and advancement. The conflict between life and work is very acute. This directly hampers them from developing their talented professionals and restricts their intellect and creativity.

Third, outdated ideas on the part of the women teachers themselves form another obstacle. This is actually the biggest subjective factor affecting them. From the perspectives of history and tradition, the difficulty for women to become talented professionals lies in the fact that history has set up more obstacles in the female development process than in the male's. Through thousands of years of social evolution and change, the historically erroneous concept that "men take care of matters outside the home while women take care of matters inside the home" gradually emerged. Today, large numbers of women are no longer proving their value only by playing the housewife role but are showing their high worth in the home and in society simultaneously. However, old-fashioned social ideas cannot be eradicated in a brief time. Some women teachers lack confidence in their own ability and success, believe themselves to be inferior to men, and lack the courage and determination to compete with them. Subjectively, they believe that becoming talented professionals is men's business and their hope for career success is pinned on their husbands and children. They have a displaced success mentality, or are complacent because of it. This "great" sacrificing spirit ruthlessly "deprives" them of their ideals and pursuit of becoming talented professionals.

HOW WOMEN TEACHERS CAN BECOME TALENTED PROFESSIONALS

"All society should establish a civilized and progressive concept of women" was a notion put forward by Comrade Jiang Zemin in his address to the meeting commemorating the eightieth anniversary of the "March 8th Women's Day." The purpose is to create a very favorable social and cultural environment for the healthy development of Chinese women. From the perspective of women's development, they should also have fine psychological qualities.

First, women teachers should have the ambition to become talented professionals. Whether women teachers in higher educational institutions can become talented professionals depends on whether they can face up to and overcome the difficulties caused by their physiology. Otherwise, there is no other option. They must, therefore, shake off the restrictions of traditional ideas, overcome such mental blocks as inferiority and dependency, establish high ideals and aspirations, and make their utmost effort to become talented professionals for the sake of building socialist modernization with Chinese characteristics. The famous writer Gorky had said: "The higher one sets one's goal, the faster his talents will develop." Only by setting lofty goals can women teachers in higher education bring their intellectual and nonintellectual factors into play to realize their goal of becoming talented professionals, fully display their creativity and imagination, overcome hardships in their path, acquire self-respect, self-confidence, and self-reliance, and make self-improvement.

Second, they must have firm career aspirations. Careers are created by human beings. People with careers must have firm ambitions. As the great ancient man of letters, Su Shi, said: "All who do great things in history not only possess extraordinary talent, but also unshakable will." Will is not only expressed in the pursuit of one's career, but also in being fearless and daring in the face of hardship. At present, as new types of higher educational institutions are being established, the form, level, and specialization of schools are changing in keeping with the human resource demand in the market. To adapt to these changes, the knowledge of women teachers must have depth and breadth. This means that women teachers must break out of the confines of the school, predict the human resource requirements of the market, analyze the changes and future of the areas of specialization, overcome all difficulties, and expand their knowledge reserve.

Third, women must actively participate in research. They should undertake cutting-edge research in interdisciplinary sciences. Such women teachers not only must have a solid grounding in basic theory and the ability to make breakthroughs, they must also be absorbed in their research and not be affected by short-term material incentives. Geared to the main battlefield of economic construction, they should utilize their intellectual superiority and directly serve economic construction through research. This requires them to have broad knowledge and to pay attention to training and improving their ability to solve practical problems. Under the conditions of a market economy, they must establish the concept of the commercialization of knowledge; in popularizing and transforming the fruits of their research, they should have knowledge of the market. This means that they have to learn the basic knowledge and develop the ability to engage in economic activity.

All walks of society should try to resolve problems for women teachers and help them do a good job in resolving the home-talent conflict. This contradiction has tormented countless thousands of men and women with aspirations from time immemorial, and especially women. In public opinion, men can be excused for not doing housework, but women doing less housework is unforgivable. Some Western psychologists have set forth the "noncompatibility law of femininity and achievement." They use statistics to show that femininity and achievement are completely incompatible. Aside from the fallacy of this "law" in statistical terms, facts have shown that a woman's determination for career attainment cannot be snuffed out. As long as women with families are firm, they can overcome all difficulties and resolve the conflict between femininity and achievement. We should take concrete action for women teachers, such as: (1) Public opinion and the men in the families must actively create conditions to help women become talented professionals. There should be a reasonable division of work at home, and housework should be shared by husband and wife. (2) Welfare programs should be expanded to take care of children and the elderly so that women do not have to worry about them. (3) Social services should be expanded. This includes, for instance, provision of prepared foods to relieve women from cooking and giving them more time to devote to teaching and research. (4) Equal competition between the sexes should be advocated. Under the same conditions, there should be no discrimination against women and they should be given fair competition opportunities. (5) Finally, school resource management units should actively create conditions to send women teachers to study and train abroad.

(Editor-in-charge: Liang Hongyi)

In: Chinese Women and the Teaching Profession
Editors: Julia Kwong and Ma Wanhua

ISBN 978-1-59033-916-9
© 2009 Nova Science Publishers, Inc.

Chapter 7

DISCUSSING WOMEN TEACHERS BECOMING TALENTED PROFESSIONALS IN HIGHER EDUCATION[*]

Huang Xuemei

Nanjing Teachers University, China

In old China, women were more repressed, inhibited, and persecuted than men. Women who made contributions to human culture were as scarce as morning stars. This is an issue that needs to be studied and explored. To speed up China's pace of reform, we must improve the cultural quality of the whole population, which naturally includes the development utilization of the intellectual ability of women, who make up nearly half of the population. Women teachers in higher educational institutions are a special occupational group. Whether they can become truly talented professionals and fully utilize their intelligence and abilities is a very important question. This article explores this issue from personal experience and observation.

THE NEED FOR WOMEN TEACHERS IN HIGHER EDUCATION TO BECOME TALENTED PROFESSIONALS

Like their male counterparts, the needs of women teachers in higher education are varied. Their primary needs are conditions for survival such as food, clothing, shelter, and transportation. Behind that is the need for stable work and other safeguards. Then come love, friendship, and a family. They wish to have friends—to have healthy and sincere friendships and communication with others in a collective and with colleagues. When faced with difficulties, they wish to have the concern and help of the collective and their comrades and the latter's support and encouragement in work. They also hope to obtain the same stable status as male teachers, to get an accurate and fair evaluation of themselves from others, and to possess self-respect and dignity as well as respect from others. If these needs cannot be

---

[*] Translation © 2000 M.E. Sharpe, Inc., from the Chinese text. Huang Xuemei, "Yu gaoxiao nujiaoshi tan chengcai."

minimally fulfilled, they become weaker and more filled with feelings of inferiority than males. Compared with males, their primary needs occupy a relatively important place. Especially after having children, they are bound by their sense of security and motherly love, which take up more of their energy. When these basic needs are fulfilled, they also have higher-level needs—self-realization or the wish to become talented professionals, the hope that their potential and abilities can be further developed and utilized. While doing a good job in their teaching, they would squeeze time out to engage in research and to write treatises and other works to realize their need to become talented professionals.

THE IMPACT OF WOMEN TEACHERS' AGE ON BECOMING TALENTED PROFESSIONALS

The age of women teachers in higher education has two meanings—physiological age and years of teaching experience. For the sake of convenience, we shall discuss the typical case when the two ages coincide—that is, older teachers with longer teaching experience, middle-aged teachers with relatively long teaching experience, and younger teachers with little teaching experience. Women teachers at these different levels have different age characteristics.

With the progression of age, older women teachers undergo marked physiological changes, including decreasing function of the sensory organs, slowing down of movement, etc. At the same time, their mental state also undergoes an obvious change: they are stable in their work and deeply love teaching. This "stability" and "love" have profound sociological and psychological underpinnings. The majority, having gone through the vicissitudes of life and experienced different social systems, have a profound love of the socialist education system and are especially appreciative of their present hard-earned teaching job. They are especially concerned about contributions they should make to society in their later years. They are constantly trying to improve themselves on the job and diligently, reliably, and prudently dedicate their lives to education. They have a strong sense of professional integrity. In their many years of teaching, they have formed lofty professional ethics and become clearly "student-oriented." Their fondest hope is that their students would excel. In addition, they are strongly defensive. Because of their unusual life experiences, they are prudent in talk and action and usually in a defensive mood. It must be pointed out that this feature has negative effects on their becoming talented professionals.

The characteristic of middle-aged women teachers is their enterprising spirit. They have relatively solid knowledge of their specialty and want to move ahead in their careers. At the same time, they have a strong sense of confidence and competitiveness and are sure of their own abilities. After completing their regular teaching assignments, they put extra pressure on themselves; and driven by competitiveness, they forge ahead to achieve their goals. However, they feel different degrees of repression: they feel that despite their efforts in teaching and other undertakings, their expectations and hopes in such areas as rank, salary, and benefits have not been fulfilled due to many restrictions. This causes them to feel repressed when facing setbacks. This kind of pressure, if correctly guided, could become a motivation to excel, and actually constitutes one of their advantages.

Because of their short time on the job, young women teachers lack a sense of stability. When faced with difficulties and setbacks in teaching, they are lull of misgivings and discouraged. With time, they will gradually adjust their behavior and overcome this problem. Another characteristic is their ambition and eagerness to become talented professionals; they study hard, dare to explore, and actively participate in education reform. They are energetic and thirsty for knowledge. Driven by their ideals, they pay attention to the improvement of their educational theory and knowledge. They often set up momentous and lofty goals for themselves, hoping to train themselves to he qualified teachers in a short time. This shows their simplistic thinking, overlooking the difficulties in becoming talented professionals, as well as their potential and basis for becoming talented professionals.

We have analyzed the ability, quality, and conditions for becoming talented professionals among the older, middle-aged, and young women teacher groups. We can see that women teachers of all ages have the potential to excel. The important thing is to correctly handle the relationship between age characteristics and becoming a talented professional.

CONDITIONS FOR WOMEN TEACHERS TO BECOME TALENTED PROFESSIONALS

There are many conditions for women teachers in higher education to become talented professionals. They can roughly be grouped into external conditions and internal (inherent) conditions.

External Conditions

External conditions refer to the environment of women teachers in higher educational institutions. This includes the natural and social environments. The social environment has the main impact on developing talented professionals. The social environment can be divided into the large environment, the subenvironment, and the small environment, or the geographical area, the work unit, and the home.

From ancient times, the conditions for women teachers to become talented professionals are closely related to the political, economic, and cultural characteristics of the large environment. Today, in particular, political equality and progress, economic prosperity and development, and the extent of development of cultural and scientific levels have a decisive influence on women teachers becoming talented professionals. Their subenvironment is also very important. For instance, the composition of the personnel, the qualifications of the human resources, the conditions for teaching and research, and the quality of the equipment and instruments in the work unit all directly affect the possibility and progress of their becoming talented professionals.

Every person lives in a home. What can the small environment of the home offer women teachers in higher education? This depends on how the individual handles the question. There is no home in the world that will provide ready conditions for becoming a talented professional. History tells us that both wealthy families with excellent conditions and impoverished families with poor conditions have produced all kinds of outstanding talents.

However, the situation of family—good or bad—such as the ideological and political viewpoints, moral and ethical level, the professional ability of family members, the family structure, and financial and living standards each have a direct influence on the possibility of women teachers becoming talented professionals. Among family relationships, that between husband and wife is the closest. There is nothing more important in the mutual understanding of a couple than their views regarding careers. For instance, there are many couples in which both spouses have taken off in their careers and they encourage, support, and help each other in their work. Such understanding, support, and encouragement in each other's careers is no doubt an indispensable support that women teachers need if they are to excel. Other family relationships also have different effects on a person's becoming a talented professional.

In sum, the external environment provides the objective conditions for and has an important impact on the ability of women teachers at higher educational institutions to become successful professionals. However, external conditions are not the decisive factors. The growth of a person is governed by many factors and is the result of the interaction of internal and external factors. The external environment can only exert a decisive impact when it is in harmony and consistent with the internal environment.

Internal Conditions

There are many internal conditions necessary for women teachers in higher education to become talents. First, a healthy physiological and mental quality is one of the bases for becoming a talented professional.

A healthy physique is an indispensable material precondition for becoming a talented professional. Relatively speaking, the female physiology is superior to the male's in some respects. For instance, from the perspective of modern immunology, since the genes responsible for producing immunological substances are mainly contained in the X chromosome, the female body possesses twice the amount of these substances than the male. The female body also contains a much higher amount of M-immunoglobulins, which give the female a stronger immunity against viral infections. In addition, the function of the female immune system degenerates slower than the male's. They thus have a stronger resistance to many forms of disease, including cancer. These physiological advantages give females more favorable conditions for becoming talented professionals.

The psychological conditions for becoming talented professionals can be divided into intellectual and nonintellectual factors. The same applies to women teachers in higher education. The intellectual factors generally include five areas—attention, observation, imagination, thinking, and memory. Attention enables the concentration of mental activities as one prepares for teaching and research, and can raise the efficiency of a person's observation, memory, imagination, and thinking. We know that people who have a high level of concentration seem to have opened a skylight to intelligence. A teacher's attention to his or her profession is closely related to the attainment of his or her optimum ability. A women teacher can achieve the maximum extent of her ability only when her full attention is concentrated in her teaching. Facts prove that the attention of women teachers in higher education is very intense. In an initial survey of 106 relatively successful women teachers in a certain university, we found that 97 of these, or over 92 percent, had made some achievements and were known for their teaching and research. In summing up their road to becoming talents, they all emphasized the relationship between their concentration and educational occupation. They felt that such concentration helped them to improve their knowledge, adjust their interests and hobbies, and add to the effective use of time and energy.

A high degree of and a keen observation is indispensable to people who have made great accomplishments in history. This is especially advantageous to women teachers in higher education in their classroom teaching. They have the merits of clear speech, distinct enunciation, gentle and moving tone, strong expressive power, lively presentation, and the ability to energize the class. At the same time, they are good at observing things. In order to get the best results in teaching, a women teacher constantly pays attention to the expressions and emotions revealed on the faces of students to get feedback and to measure how interested they are and how well they are receiving her words, then analyzes the situation and adjusts flexibly. Only when the teacher's and students' emotions fully commingle can students like what they hear and take in what the teacher says and can ideal teaching results be gained. If in the classroom the teacher ignores students' reactions and facial expressions and talks on and on about what he or she is interested in, the teacher is making students "take an airplane ride" (students do not understand) and naturally cannot get satisfactory teaching results.

Nonintellectual factors primarily refer to emotions, willpower, and personality. Throughout time, many famous women scientists and educators in China or abroad have possessed very high intelligence and strong emotions, a persistent willpower, and an independent personality. It is hard to imagine that a person who lacks persistence and is reluctant to put in hard work can accomplish anything.

DIFFICULTIES IN WOMEN TEACHERS BECOMING TALENTED PROFESSIONALS AND MEASURES TO OVERCOME THEM

We should recognize both the many favorable conditions for women teachers at higher educational institutions to become talented professionals as well as the many difficulties and obstacles in their path. We have to face them and adopt corresponding measures to overcome them. Only then can we do a better job of guiding and helping women teachers to become talents.

Difficulties in the Way of Becoming Talented Professionals

Difficulties in the way of women teachers becoming talents come first of all from social prejudices against women. The traditional and feudal ideas of the "three obediences and four virtues" and the saying that "it is a virtue for women to be without talent" bind women hand and foot like invisible cords and cause their spirit to be greatly repressed. Society's low expectations of women also cause them to feel inferior and increase the impediments to their becoming talents. People expect men to gain greater achievements in every field where success is possible, and give praise to successful males. They do not have the same expectations of women. Frequently, people expect men to accomplish great things, but not necessarily women. This reflects the prejudice against women as talented professionals. Second, the bias of some family members' add to their difficulties. They feel that women teachers in higher education can only be at home as "dutiful wives and good mothers" and have no need to be successful career women. Hence they give no encouragement or support to the women's career pursuits aid commitments, and even try to keep women from pursuing them. For instance, some parents-in-law demand daughters-in-law to obey and satisfy their every wish. Some husbands demand their wives to help them in their careers as well as take care of the home. Children demand their mothers to be good tutors in their studies and good nannies at home. Housework often lies so heavily on women teachers' shoulders that they have no breathing space and have to give up their spare-time studies and advanced training. This directly affects their chances for becoming talented professionals. Third, some women have a problem in their understanding of themselves and their self-confidence. For instance, some bend under the effect of old traditional education and social opinion. Some lack confidence in their own ability and success, believing themselves to be inferior to male teachers and lacking the spirit to challenge the latter. Some lack necessary courage and decisiveness and an independent and innovative spirit and often bow to external pressures and give in to their own inertia, thus giving up the pursuit of their career goals and even the best time of their lives to become talented professionals. Some young women teachers, after getting married, having children, and having to take care of the home, objectively have no time to pursue becoming talents. Subjectively, they think that "to become talented professionals is men's business; I am after all a women and my primary responsibility is to be a good wife and mother." They thus set unduly low goals in their academic careers and put their hopes instead on their husbands and children, thus generating a mentality of "displaced success," with which they are quite satisfied. They are thus willing to dedicate and quietly sacrifice themselves for the family, and become "dutiful wives and good mothers" in fact as well as in name. This is precisely the "great" sacrificing spirit that mercilessly "deprives" them of their ideals and their pursuit of becoming talented, and is the major obstacle standing in the way of their becoming talented professionals.

Measures to be Adopted

In view of the difficulties and obstacles faced by women teachers in higher education in becoming talented, we can generally take two types of measures. Society should eliminate the hurdles and create favorable conditions for women teachers to raise their expectations, affirm their goals, and to carry them out, so that women would devote more time and energy to education. This includes, for instance, advocating equal competition and nondiscrimination against women, increasing social welfare benefits, setting up homes for the elderly and kindergartens, etc., so as to relieve women teachers of their worries at home. In regard to the service industries, society should increase services to relieve the domestic chores of women teachers so that they would have more time for teaching and self-improvement.

In addition, women teachers' own attitude towards these difficulties and obstacles is essential. They must adopt corresponding measures to improve their attitudes.

First, they should have strong self-confidence and motivation. Ideals and beliefs point to the direction in the development of talent and are its spiritual support. Motivation and the pursuit of excellent form the internal driving force. Since ancient times, stories of women rising to prominence from obscurity demonstrate that their extraordinary contributions came from their contempt for social prejudice and determination to "compete with men." The first woman member of the Chinese Academy of Sciences, the world-renowned obstetrician-gynecologist Liu Qiaozhi, is one such great woman who possesses strong motivation and confidence. She has never been one to draw back.

In a survey of 150 women teachers of higher educational institutions, we found that 84 percent considered themselves active, motivated, and committed to blazing new trails; and 77 percent wanted their leaders to give them more assignments and wanted to be successful in their teaching. From this it can be seen that women teachers are capable of breaking through any feelings of inferiority to replace them with self-confidence and an enterprising spirit.

Second, women teachers must have an indomitable willpower and perseverance. An indomitable willpower and perseverance are even more important to the broad masses of women teachers in higher education in becoming talented professionals. Due to physiological reasons, women shoulder the important task of reproduction to propagate the human race and are therefore not as "continuous" and "sustained" as men in their work. In addition, their mid-life transition comes earlier than men's and the effects last longer. These factors cause special problems for women. Moreover, because of gaps related to sociohistorical reasons and physiological characteristics, the female willpower is generally weaker and women may sometimes be overwhelmed by difficulties. Some, for instance, will give up their original plans due to housework or weak constitutions. That is why an indomitable willpower and perseverance constitute a greater test and higher demand for women.

In the history of science, the seven women who have won the Nobel Prize prove that only people with indomitable willpower can ascend to the heights of science. The Polish scientist Madam Marie Curie, who twice won the Nobel Prize, was the discoverer of radium, thus shaking to the core the once all-powerful classical physics and chemistry concept and principles. She was doubted by conventional scientists and even attacked and challenged. Faced with these challenges, Madam Curie and husband Pierre Curie, through hard work and numerous experiments, eventually extracted radium and discovered its atomic weight, giving a scientific response to all who challenged her authority. She had said with deep feeling: "One must never give in to any person or difficulty." She thus created a glorious example in the history of talented professional women.

Third, women must eliminate external interference and go against the current. The broad mass of Chinese women, subjected to 2,000 years of traditional prejudices such as "men are the principals and women the followers," are apt to have feelings of inferiority, lagging behind, and dependence. These are all cancers invading their ability to become talented professionals. They infect each other in a vicious cycle and hamper to a great extent women's growth into talented professionals. Some women teachers are in the adverse situation of facing opposition from their families. Some women teachers with the will to become talented professionals are able to reconcile different kinds of personal conflicts when faced with difficulties and interference. They dare to sweep away all interference and immerse themselves totally in the cause of education with a broad embrace. They overlook all personal gains and losses and all trivial matters unrelated to their goal of becoming talented professionals and concentrate totally on delving into their teaching—to doing a good job each time they teach in class and nurture every college student. This spirit is worth advocating. Folk wisdom has it that "it is hard to be a woman." To be a woman teacher in higher education with aspirations and talents is even harder. At this time of reform and opening in the country, education must develop and adapt to the needs of economic development. This means that the role of women teachers in higher education must be fully developed. Hence, it is our hope that all society can adopt an active attitude and give diligent support and assistance to women teachers and women technical specialists to enable them to become talented professionals so that they use their abilities and potential to make greater contributions to the fostering of talents in higher education.

PART IV: ROLE CONFLICT

In: Chinese Women and the Teaching Profession
Editors: Julia Kwong and Ma Wanhua

ISBN 978-1-59033-916-9
© 2009 Nova Science Publishers, Inc.

Chapter 8

ESSENCE OF THE "QUANDARY OF THE MULTIPLE ROLES OF WOMEN TEACHERS IN CHINA'S HIGHER EDUCATIONAL INSTITUTIONS"*

Huang Huifang

China Women's Education Research Center,
Huazhong Science and Engineering University, Wuhan, China

The theory of women's liberation is a pluralistic ideological system. Women of different nations, races, classes, and ages, due to different social experiences, have different theories of women's liberation. The nature and complexity of the occupation of women teachers in higher educational institutions determine their characteristics among intellectual career women, the high standard and level of their demand for liberation, as well as the special characteristics of their theory. It is indeed meaningful to analyze the essence of the quandary of this social group in regard to their roles.

Women Teachers' Role Quandary is the Early Awakening and Exploration of Subjective Consciousness

The important position and role of higher education in the modernization of society is becoming increasingly significant and recognized. The aim and mission of higher education is to promote social progress and the overall development of human beings. At a time when we are crossing to a new century, the demand on higher education is more pluralistic. Higher educational institutions should try hard to become the "incubators" of new and high technology industries, the "development unit" for high-level human resources, and the "think tank" for drawing up scientific policies. The many demands on teachers from society, students, and parents are gender neutral: that is to say, women teachers in higher education bear the same occupational pressures as male teachers. The teaching profession requires individuals to have intelligence, wide-ranging knowledge, and superior speaking and research abilities. These demands add greater sense of urgency, crisis, participation, and achievement

---

* Translation © 2000 M.E. Sharpe, Inc., from the Chinese text. Huang Huifang, "Lun 'Zhongguo gaoxiao nujiaoshi duochongjiaose kunhuo' zhi shizhi," *Shanghai gaoxiao yanjiu (jiaoyu luntan)* (Studies on Shanghai's Higher Education [Education Forum]), no. 5, 1996.

among women teachers. The college campus environment provides some advantages in that the sense of gender equality is stronger with less gender discrimination compared with other sectors of society. Generally, as long as the women teachers try, they can all become talented professionals. So we can also call colleges and universities special zones for women to become talented professionals. However, we cannot ignore the disadvantages. First, in schools, the heads of administration at all levels are generally male, and in their ideology and concepts men like to make evaluations and choices on the basis of their own physiological category. They cannot bear women whose individual characters and abilities are stronger than men's. Second, although women teachers do not consider child-bearing as the only theme in their life's cycle, for most it is one of life's major journeys. Child-bearing and rearing take up a fairly large portion of a women's time and energy, and in an age when knowledge is constantly being updated, this will cause a certain gap between them and male teachers. Third, women college teachers undertake more housework than males. According to one article, of the 2,301 women teachers in one science and engineering university (37.8 percent of the total number of teachers in that school), there were 371, or 24.2 percent, at and above the rank of associate professor, and 85 percent of these also took care of such matters as grocery shopping, making meals, washing clothes, and cleaning at home. Of the women teachers, 50 percent managed family finance and tutored children in studies; 32.5 percent also took care of elderly people in the family; and 34.6 percent did other miscellaneous work. Women teachers in higher education may put all of their dedication toward their families, husbands, and children and they would be quite satisfied, but their profession does not allow them to do so. The above-mentioned survey also found that in the question "attitude to career and family," 39.3 percent chose "putting career first"; 57.4 percent chose "putting career and family on equal footing"; 0.8 percent chose "putting the family first"; and 2.5 percent chose "putting personal pleasures first." This shows that the majority of the women teachers place career and family on the same footing, and that the dual role is entirely their own choice. In real life, when career and family come into conflict, they always try to preserve both and survive the storm. This is precisely the greatness and sacrificing spirit of the female gender. Humans are constantly living amidst worries. The worries of intellectuals are greater than other people. Those of women teachers in higher education are still greater. These worries constitute both their dilemma and agony.

The higher the education received, the higher the self-expectation and the stronger the wish to utilize one's potential and creativity. Women teachers in higher education are not reconciled to be submerged by family and housework, but they would not chose a road antagonistic to their husbands and families either. They do not have to have a showdown with their husbands because in the Chinese family, especially in families of intellectual women in particular, these women are no longer dominated by male rights but have equal rights. Most of the women teachers live in harmony with their husbands, going ahead hand in hand and sharing the housework.

Since the dual roles of intellectual women are their own choice, why are they sometimes in a quandary? This is because (1) although intellectual women choose a dual role, they still get frustrated in real life when they encounter problems; (2) they want to raise an outcry to undermine women's role in housework and the mentality that "men take care of matters outside the home and women take care of matters inside the home"; and (3) women like to complain in order to keep their own equilibrium. Once they pass this stage, they are no longer bothered. This author moderated meetings in which she personally observed that female mentors of Ph.D. students and women professors did not seem to be bothered in this respect. This is a sign of their resolve and maturity.

"ROLE QUANDARY" CONFORMS TO THE LOGIC OF THE HISTORY OF THE WOMEN'S LIBERATION MOVEMENT IN CHINA

"Role quandary" is the mindset of women teachers, and in a certain sense it is a trend of the period. There are different manifestations of mindset during different historical periods. It is extremely meaningful to observe the changes in this mindset and look for the laws that govern it.

Stage of Relative Stability during the More than 2,000 Years of Feudal Society

In feudal society, women were confined to a single role at home. The invisible atmosphere and subliminal influence of norms and rites nurtured the thinking and behavior of women. This powerful molding led women to observe the rites to the extent of even dying to defend their honor. They did it willingly and happily, filled with a sense of moral righteousness. Since "sacrifice" could win the praise of society and of public opinion, their minds were at ease. In addition, although the imprisoned heart felt pain being confined at home with no (or little) contact with the outside world, the imprisoned heart, though pained, it was still relatively stable. This was the general situation.

Stage of Tumult: Contemporary Times Around the May fourth Movement (1919)

The women's liberation movement in China "had always been tied to the Chinese revolution." During the Great Revolution, women's associations advocated by women leaders of the Guomindang and Communist Party such as Song Qingling, Cai Chang, Deng Yingchao, and He Xiangning were very active. In the three townships of Wuhan, for instance, spirited, energetic, and hard working women trainers in party affairs went to the factories, schools, neighborhoods, and rural areas to carry out revolutionary publicity and mobilize people to participate in the revolutionary struggle against imperialism and feudalism. During this period, the mindset of Chinese women turned from stability to fluctuation, from being consistent to conflictual, and from equilibrium to disequilibrium. The woman of this time was characterized by the pursuit of survival and the winning of minimal personal rights and freedoms. However, the traditional criterion of a woman being a "dutiful wife and good mother" who only look care of matters inside the home was not yet criticized.

Postdevelopment Stage of Stability: From Liberation to the Eve of Reform and the Open Policy

During this relatively long period, the broad masses of women happily walked out the doors of their homes and became "half the sky" in every field of endeavor. In those exciting and stimulating years, women became their own masters. They went to work during the day and did overtime to take care of children at night without complaints. Their mindset was especially good. This author spent a few years in a military factory and found that many of the women workers wanted nothing except "to make contributions" to society. They seldom considered their personal interests and did not feel that "men are superior to women." "Complacency brings happiness" reflected the stable mindset of the women as a group during that period.

New Stage of Tumult: Postreform and the Open Policy

With reform, opening, and the transformation of the economic system, deep fractures occurred in the traditional value system. In the transition to new ideas, women's mindset, such as those of women workers being laid off from enterprises before retirement age, has suffered great shocks. The mindset of women teachers in higher education has always been very sensitive and easily shaken in the storms of reform. They have never had such a strong wish as they do today to flap their wings and soar to the skies like eagles.

Learning to Survive: Modern Society and Chinese Cultural Background Require Women Teachers to Integrate Multiple Roles

Because Chinese women's liberation was tied to the overall Chinese revolution right from the start, men and women should advance together shoulder to shoulder. This author is therefore of the opinion that a good solution to the role quandary should be sought from the cultural characteristics of China. The quintessence of Chinese culture is the spirit of harmony *(he he)*—nature, society, the individual, the soul, and civilization are all in harmony. The role quandary of women teachers arises from the conflict between the individual and society, individual and individual, and within the soul of the individual. The spirit of harmony is to be born, to exist, to reach, to establish, and to love together. This of course also applies to the harmony in the many roles in one's soul.

China is a culture that values family. Although there are defects in the patriarchal society of the past, the "harmony" and "happiness" reflected in the family is beneficial to social security. Thus, a woman who has self-respect, self-confidence, and self-reliance and makes self-improvement, a capable woman with high quality all around, can never be a success in her career but at the same time be a shrew at home (shrews are on the increase in society). This author, after interviewing a number of women professors and supervisors of doctoral student in higher education, discovered that they were not only widely knowledgeable and admired for their lofty personalities, their female gentleness and deep emotions were also respected and cherished by their students. One of the teaching research groups in the math department (higher math) of a science and engineering university possesses an outstanding group of mainly women teachers. They receive many teaching awards every year. They treat their students with discipline and maternal love, and they unite with their colleagues in harmony, showing the special characteristics of women.

In modern society, the attempt to assume only one easy, single role is no longer possible. Both men and women have to relearn how to survive. A person with a rich personality and overall development must undertake different responsibilities, which means different (and multiple) roles. Take a look around you: Is not every man or woman, young or old, taking on multiple roles? The socialization process of each individual is the process in which, with the increase in responsibilities, he or she assumes ever more roles.

(Editor-in-charge: Xiao Qingzhang)

REFERENCES

Bao Xiaolan, chief editor. "Study and Evaluation of Western Feminism." Life-Reading-New Knowledge Sanlian Bookstore, 1995 ed.

Gong Fang and Mao Rong. "Reflections as we Face a New Era and Future Prospects," *Gaodeng jiaoyu yanjiu* (Higher Education Research), no. 4, 1995.

Yu Rongpei. "The Multiple Roles of Higher Women Intellectuals and Recommendations on How to Handle the Issue." Paper presented at the "Women and Education Symposium" (Wuhan). June 1995.

Zhang Liwen. "The Harmonious Union Spirit in Chinese Culture and the 21st Century." *Xueshu yuekan* (Academic Monthly), no. 9, 1995.

In: Chinese Women and the Teaching Profession
Editors: Julia Kwong and Ma Wanhua

ISBN 978-1-59033-916-9
© 2009 Nova Science Publishers, Inc.

Chapter 9

WOMEN TEACHERS' ROLE CONFLICT AND ITS MANAGEMENT[*]

Liu Jianling

Role is how social psychologists express an individual's position and status in the system of social relationships.

The social role of women teachers as modem career women in a multidimensional life of the social, school, family, and personal areas has a multiple character. This multiplicity will necessarily cause role conflicts because of the different demands of the different roles. Such multiple role conflicts will inevitably have a major impact on the work, study, and life of women teachers. This article will explore this issue.

EXPRESSIONS OF WOMEN TEACHERS' ROLE CONFLICTS

In modern Chinese society, the social position and qualifications of women teachers have improved greatly. This does not mean that traditional women's issues have all been resolved. Instead, the traditional female role and the modern professional role have acquired new properties characteristic of the times, and these characteristics necessarily result in new role conflicts and contradictions. The concrete manifestations of the role conflicts of women teachers are [addressed below].

Conflict in Role Expectations

Role expectation refers to the hopes and demands of society, others, and oneself about the role one plays. Since no one undertakes merely one single role, there are many role

---

[*] Translation © 2000 M.E. Sharpe, Inc., from the Chinese text. Liu Jianling, "Nujiaoshide jiaose chongtu yu guanli," *Jiangxi jiaoyu xueyuan xuebao* (Jingxi Education College Journal), vol. 14 (general no. 50), no. 4 (1993).

expectations, and to satisfy all of them is hard. Thus conflicts and contradictions inevitably arise. The conflicts are mainly expressed in subjective and objective ways.

A. Conflict of Objective Role Expectations

On the one hand, the professional role of women teachers is the educator's role, and this is society's primary expectation of women teachers. The more developed the society and its science and technology, the more conspicuous the role of teachers and the higher the demand and expectations of society toward the teachers. In terms of professional ethics, society asks teachers to have high morals and ethical standards, be true to the cause of education, love their students, and wholeheartedly dedicate their lives to the growth of the new generation. The complexity and creative character of teachers' labor demand that they have wide knowledge, varied interests, and multiple talents; and that they possess both specialized knowledge, educational theory, and teaching ability. The extensive character and continuity of teachers' labors also demand that teachers have a strong sense of responsibility and seize all opportunities to secure time and space for education. The infinite possibilities in human development demand infinite time on the part of teachers. In short, lofty morals and ethics, an independent and forward-looking consciousness, a fine character, wide knowledge, and varied talents are the objective expectations of teachers from society. To a woman, these demands can only be reached with enormous effort.

On the other hand, the woman teacher also has to fulfill her gender role in family relations. Women have always been responsible for the human reproductive function—to give birth to children as wife and mother. All these activities have been carried on inside the home, and that is why some people also call the female role their family role. As a woman, she is the center of the family and has to spend a great deal of time and energy on household labor. In real life, husbands want wives to be sweet and gentle, virtuous and understanding: they do not want wives to be too capable and to stand out from the crowd. They hope that wives have a sense of dependence on husbands so that the marriage relationship can reach equilibrium and stability. As a mother, a woman is required to have the heart of a loving mother and to be concerned with the daily life, study, and development of her children and to preserve the purity and dedication of motherly love. In the traditional family, a woman also has to be the filial daughter-in-law to her parents-in-law, to be obedient to them and to handle all kinds of other in-law relationships well. In short, the traditional female role requires a woman to be sweet, gentle, and docile and to revolve around the family. However, a woman's time and energy is limited and she often finds it hard to play both the role of "teacher" and of "woman," thus giving rise to a certain imbalance between the two. Relaxing their hold on either side will bring dissatisfaction and cause the women teachers themselves to lose their mental equilibrium.

B. Conflict of Subjective Role Expectations

Everybody wants a perfect life. As women's sense of independence rises, they hope to be successful in their careers without losing marriage and family. Women teachers are no exceptions. Many teachers have high hopes in their careers and hope to reflect their own social worth in the course of this pursuit, build up an independent character, and break away from mediocrity and ignorance. At the same time, they also need a happy relationship in their marriage and deep bonds with their children. They must spend enormous time and energy to gain all this, because each wish is bound up with responsibilities and obligations and can only be won through work and effort. Women teachers, however, do not have a lot of time and energy, and in fact, they have less time and energy due to physiological limitations. Thus, there exist many conflicts and contradictions if women teachers want to do well in both career and family. As a nationally outstanding class monitor said: "The time and energy of an individual is limited, but as a good teacher, responsibility and obligation are unlimited. As a good mother and wife, the responsibility and obligation are also unlimited. To get two unlimited's from one limited can only arouse a lot of contradictions and conflicts."

Conflict in Role Status

Role status refers to the rights enjoyed by a particular role. A gap exists between the rights enjoyed by women teachers legally and theoretically and the rights they enjoy in real life. Hence, the role conflict of women teachers is also reflected in the contradiction and gap in their role status.

A. The Gap between a Teacher's Political and Financial Position

The social position of the teacher's role is generally expressed by his or her political and financial roles. The Communist Party and government have always paid attention to the development of education and have repeatedly emphasized the importance of education for the national economy. Ideas such as "in developing the economy, education leads the way" are deeply ingrained in people's minds. The entire society understands the importance of educational development and the importance of the teaching profession. Teachers are respected by society and by the people and their political position has improved greatly. Their financial position also has improved. For many reasons, however, in real life in recent years the income of teachers has dropped compared with other professions. Moreover, the incomes of teachers and government workers are at the lowest levels. This clear gap between political position and financial position has seriously harmed the work enthusiasm of the broad masses of teachers and the stability of the teaching ranks. Not long ago, an outstanding young woman teacher who was elected as a deputy to the National People's Congress said in a newspaper interview: "When a person's financial income affects that person's human dignity, it makes one wonder if his or her career choice is worth it." This shows that even women cannot avoid the role conflict and mental quandary arising from the gap between the financial and political status of teachers.

B. The Gap between Legal Gender Equality and Actual Gender Equality

With the birth of a New China, the law affirmed women's equality with men in all areas and the party and government repeatedly emphasized protection of women's rights and forbade discrimination against women. Despite all these steps, inequality is rife in real life and discrimination and ostracism of talented women are common. There is discrimination against and suppression of female talent in student enrollment, distribution, hiring, retirement, and organizational restructuring [by laying off the less qualified ones]. These include work-unit regulations which stipulate that women workers will not have a housing allocation and cannot enjoy welfare benefits; and the grades required for hiring women are sometimes dozens of points higher or double that of men. Some work units unequivocally reject women graduates. This societal gap in women's position of being legally equal but actually not equal to men is inevitably reflected in the schools.

C. The Gap between the Positions of Female and Male Teachers in School

In schools, women teachers doing the same work as men face different treatment in promotion, distribution, welfare, and retirement. For instance, some schools disallow women from participating in the allocation of living quarters or registering to get cooking gas and free medicine for children. In the evaluation of professional titles, arrangement of major teaching tasks, and the selection of grassroots leaders, women teachers do not enjoy the same rights as male teachers.

Conflict in the Self-concept of Women Teachers

With social progress and development, society is making higher demands on the professional and family roles of women teachers, making the contradictions between their multiple roles even more acute. This, together with female weaknesses formed through thousands of years of history, cause contemporary women teachers to have mental pressures and stress, causing a strong disequilibrium in their minds and leading to conflict in their self-concept.

A. Conflict between Dependence and Independence

Among modern career women, female teachers are relatively independent financially and have a stronger sense of self-reliance. However, the traditional female mindset formed over long periods of time and the enormous pressure brought to bear on them by the conflict of multiple roles in present-day life cause many women teachers to be unable to shake off the mentality of dependence on men and to a certain extent hamper them from utilizing their ability to achieve. For instance, some young women teachers with much talent and learning still wish to find husbands whose knowledge and ability exceed theirs; some women teachers when they find their careers clashing with that of their husbands, would willingly give up their own for the sake of their husbands. On the one hand, they wish to play an independent role; on the other, traditional social and family ideas consciously or unconsciously give them some degree of dependence.

B. Conflict between Self-respect and Feelings of Inferiority

Modern society demands that women teachers as professional career women should have self-respect, self-confidence, and self-reliance and make self- improvements. Due to the limitations of traditional cultural and female physiology, some women teachers still have feelings of inferiority and lack confidence. When they are challenged in work, they often doubt their ability, causing them to stop advancing and even to hang back. We can often hear the following questions which show a lack of self-confidence: "Can I, a woman, manage a school?" "This is a graduate course. Can I teach it?" "Can I shoulder the double task of a career and a family?" This is especially so when the conflict between their professional and family roles comes into sharper conflict, and some of them hesitate and shrink back. Such lack of confidence fully reveals the feelings of inferiority in modern women teachers born under the impact of traditional ideas and values. On the contrary, a man seldom doubts his own abilities.

C. Conflict between Narrowness and Openness

For a long time, the narrow family life of women had led to the narrowness of their mental space. Despite the fact that modern life and education have opened their minds and hearts, signs of narrowness can still be found. For instance, they care a lot about what other people say about them, are overly sensitive and envious, cannot keep their cool when facing setbacks, are overly emotional, etc. They often waste time and energy on trifles which add to their already heavy mental burdens.

MANAGEMENT OF THE ROLE CONFLICTS OF WOMEN TEACHERS

The above analysis demonstrates the existence of multiple role conflicts in modern women teachers. To a certain extent, it also reflects the common characteristics of modern professional and intellectual women. In view of these role conflicts and mental quandaries faced by women teachers, school administrations should consider the following concrete measures in management:

Creation of Equal Conditions in Work and Living Environments and in Competition

The leaders of some schools have prejudices against women teachers and often use the excuse that women have too much housework and heavy burdens when not giving them due consideration. Administrators even turn around and say that this is special consideration for the women. Such practices actually only enhance the mental burdens of the women and hurt their enthusiasm. Hence school leaders must correct their understanding on this issue and truly give equal treatment to the two genders and allow fair competition. They should dare to lean on capable women teachers, accurately evaluate women teachers' accomplishments, and create equal competitive conditions and work and living environments so as to relieve women teachers' pressures and burdens in work and in their minds.

Correctly Understand the Life and Experiences of Women Teachers

For a long time, people have considered childbirth to be a woman's private business and a big defect which puts women at a disadvantage in employment, promotion, and important work assignments. Women teachers are no exception. School leaders must understand the social significance of childbirth as an important link in the progression and development of human society. This is not the women teachers' private business, even less should anyone slight them because of it. Instead, people should share the difficulties caused by women teachers' childbirth and help them smoothly pass this period of disruption. They should also put themselves in the woman's place, and, together with different sectors in society, advocate fewer births and selective birth, run good nurseries and daycare centers, be solicitous about women teachers' life, and provide necessary social services to assist in household chores. This includes, for instance, the opening of laundries, supply of hot water, help in making steamed rice, setting up of nurseries and kindergartens to lighten family burdens and release women from the shackles of heavy household burdens, thus buffering the conflict and contradiction between family and career.

Srengthening Programs to Improve Women Teachers' Psychological Well-being

The establishment of a good working environment and the lightening of family burdens of women teachers are all measures to give them objective and outside help. To really resolve the role conflicts and mental quandary of women teachers, the key is in improving women teachers' sense of self and their spiritual quality—enhancing education in self-reliance and ideals, fostering their ability in many ways, especially in self-education, overcoming their psychological and mental weaknesses so that they can truly have self-respect, self-confidence, and self-reliance and make self-improvements. Only so can the ideal of overall development in society and in the family be realized.

To be Good at Allowing Women Teachers to Utilize their Strengths and Fully Motivate their Work Enthusiasm

Women teachers have unique advantages in education and teaching. Generally speaking, they are patient and painstaking, rich in emotions, and can express themselves well. These characteristics are uniquely useful in women becoming class monitors and grassroots leaders and in teaching. School administrators should understand the special qualities and abilities of women teachers and fully trust them—activating their work fervor and enthusiasm to improve the educational strength of the schools and raise education and teaching quality.

In: Chinese Women and the Teaching Profession
Editors: Julia Kwong and Ma Wanhua

ISBN 978-1-59033-916-9
© 2009 Nova Science Publishers, Inc.

Chapter 10

THE ROLE CONFLICT IN THE OCCUPATIONAL ADJUSTMENT OF FEMALE STUDENTS IN TEACHERS SCHOOLS[*]

Fan Wen-e

The Political Education Department, Nantong Specialized Teachers College,
People's Republic of China

With the popularization of compulsory nine-year education in China, the function and position of basic education has become more prominent. Concern over the role conflict in the occupational adjustment of female students in teachers schools and women teachers in junior high schools has become more significant and urgent. After carrying out a survey of groups distributed over an extensive area, we are not optimistic about the qualifications of women teachers and the conditions society has provided for them in occupational adjustment. This article shall try to analyze from different aspects and levels the role conflict in the occupational adjustment of female students in teachers schools and of women teachers.

APPEARANCE OF ROLE CONFLICT IN THE EARLY PERIOD AFTER EMPLOYMENT

Female students enrolled in teachers schools come with solid cultural foundations and strong learning potential. They are ideologically and mentally better prepared than males to become teachers. Coming from ordinary senior high schools, they adjust to teachers schools faster, and learn their specialties and consolidate their knowledge better than the male students. From a gender perspective, the ratio between male and female is normal.

After two to three years of study, they graduate with confidence, hoping to get jobs suited to their skills. However, a gap exists between what society accepts and recognizes of them

---

[*] Translation © 2000 M.E. Sharpe, Inc., from the Chinese text. Fan Wen-e, "Shizhuan nuxuesheng zhiye shiyingzhongdejiaose chongtu wenti," *Jiangsu gaojiao* (Jiangsu Higher Education), no. 4, 1997

and their own wishes and abilities. If at the time of enrollment the gender gap is not large, female students are no longer optimistic at the time of graduation and job placement. The reasons are:

A.   *Female students have the heavy task of reproduction and raising the next generation, but society is slow to recognize this fact.* With reform and opening proceeding in depth, the gradual fostering of the talent market, and the practice of mutual selection by hiring units and job-seekers, many education departments are selecting talent in the classrooms and lecture halls. The majority of work units and departments, however, adopt the following in gender selection: Under the same conditions, they want the male graduates, not the females. Even when a female graduate has better qualifications than a male, they still want the male. When there is no choice, they have to accept females. Relatively speaking, the work units in which female graduates are placed are small with poor conditions. Why do hiring units do this? Because men and women the leaders of these units believe that women will marry and have children, with maternity leave and baby-feeding time. All these create difficulties for a unit to manage.

B.   *Traditional ideas restrict development of women teachers' social role.* Women teachers who have just started work are filled with a modern woman's hopes to pursue a wonderful life and to assume the ideal role. However, popular ideas seldom concur with this wish. In real life, culture often lags behind social development. When cohorts of normal school women graduates enter society and show their individuality, they are not accepted by the majority of males. The women face problems in marriage. They are avoided even by males who supposedly have modern ideas but actually choose women of the traditional mold. The majority of female graduates from the rural areas progress from traditional to modern ideas; but after meeting setbacks gradually lose their modern and independent ideas and the courage to seek the ideal role. Seeing the trend of social selection and identification, they once again carefully pick up traditional ideas and try hard to become a woman in the traditional sense—meek, gentle, virtuous, and wise. Restricted by traditional ideas, women teachers find it very difficult to realize their social worth and develop their social role.

C.   *Inferiority and negative ideas affect women teachers' rapid growth.* Women teachers with traditional ideas often lack the inner drive that is indispensable to success. Their wish to put their potential into play to win success is constantly weakening. Surveys have shown that many women do not evaluate themselves highly, cannot see their social worth, and possess low self-esteem. In the face of challenges, they often deny their own ability before they even try, or lightly and carelessly give up their pursuits.

ROLE CONFLICT IN THE ON-THE-JOB EDUCATION OF WOMEN GRADUATES

After working for one or two years, most women teachers get married, have children, and start to assume both social and family roles. If they have a problem in social identification and self-perception in the initial period of work, then after marriage and children they face a large number of real problems in work and life. The capacities of their role have increased.

The Daughter (Daughter-in-law) and Wife in Traditional Roles

If the parents of both spouses are alive when a woman teacher sets up a family she would have to perform her filial duties as daughter-in-law and daughter. The natural sentiments of women teachers toward their parents, as compared to women in other professions, are even deeper and more inclusive. Inside traditional moral boundaries, the filial piety they show toward their parents-in-law are greater than others of their sex. According to one survey, on disputes between mothers-in-law and daughters-in-law, only 2 percent are between women teachers and their mothers-in-law. This demonstrates that women teachers are not only learned and reasonable, they also attach much importance to their moral and ethical self-cultivation and strictly follow the rules for a woman.

Women teachers also have to fulfill the role of wives "who take care of matters inside the home." In China, the traditional and natural division of work is "the man takes care of matters outside the home and the woman takes care of matters inside the home." Some people say that after marriage the woman has to "carry both her husband and cooking pots and pans on her back," Her only responsibility at home is to do a good job taking care of her husband's needs, and this is her personal duty. The results of our survey of 100 male and female secondary school teachers are as follows:

Answers to the question "Please recall the average amount of time you spent every day last week on the following activities" are shown in Table 1. They show that women teachers do more housework than male teachers, and these are concentrated in basic daily routines such as making meals and washing clothes.

Table 1. Hours spent daily on household work in a female teacher's home

Average hours per day during previous week	Husband	Wife
Average daily time making meals	0.79	1.72
Average daily time washing clothes	0.48	0.85
Average daily time taking care of children and elderly	0.09	0.12

Source: Survey conducted by the author.

In answer to the question "in which of the following areas do you think your husband (wife) needs to improve," 27 percent of the wives wished their husbands would get ahead in their careers while 11 percent of the husbands wished their wives would get ahead. At the same time, 11 percent of the wives wished their husbands would help more with housework and 26 percent of the husbands wished their wives would be more understanding. The percentages of husbands wishing their wives would make progress in their work and wives wishing husbands woul help with the housework coincide. This shows that women teachers would like their husbands to be more successful in their societal roles and take up an appropriate amount of housework, while male teachers long for their wives' understanding and wish the latter would appropriately engage in their own pursuits. The survey also found that a great many women teachers still feel guilty because they have to take less care of husband and children when busy at work.

In their role as mothers, the majority of women teachers pay a great deal of attention to and spend an enormous amount of energy on the education and nurturing of children. (See Table 2 for the survey results.) The survey showed that compared to male teachers women teachers spend thrice the time teaching their children to acquire a skill or hobby. At the same time, children expect their teacher mothers to take care of their daily needs, to provide assistance in studies, and to be a good tutor, friend, and emotional confidant. Women teachers consider the above their divine obligations. They feel guilty if they fail in this role.

The Teacher in a Modern Rote

Schools do not distinguish between female and male teachers in work arrangements and demands. Professional review bodies at the national and other levels also confer ranks and promotions on men and women teachers according to the same standards. Many women teachers fall short of their professional goals and lack confidence in competition, give up, or fail because of lack of ability.

Clashes and conflicts are inevitable given the different roles played by women teachers. These are mainly manifested in:

Table 2. Caring for children (Sample questionnaire)

	Male (hrs.)	Female (hrs.)
Daily time spent taking care of children	0.51	0.71
Daily time spent tutoring children	0.48	0.68

Source: Survey conducted by the author.

A.   *Time conflict.* Time is a constant, while work and the amount of labor is a variable. The average daily time women teachers spent making meals was 2.2 times that of male teachers, washing clothes 1.8 times greater, taking care of elders 1.3 times greater, taking care of children 1.4 times greater, and tutoring children also 1.4 times greater. In a limited time, the more the time spent on one activity, the less the time left for other activities. If more activities are squeezed into a limited time, they will necessarily come into conflict. When a dual role results in a time conflict, women teachers generally have three choices. One is to tip the scale toward the family (in other words, put the family first and career second). In the work situation, knowledge is frequently updated and interpersonal relations are tense: the family, in comparison, is a warmer and more peaceful place. Hence women choose the home to be the center of their being and give up on the development of their societal role. The second is to put family and career on par. In an attempt to spread limited energy and time on family and career, they do an average job in both. The third is to tip the scales toward career, or put career first and family second. They divide their energy in different roles in different time-spaces, trying to do well in two very different areas to find a way to be successful in their careers while building a happy home. This choice is extremely difficult on the women teachers and the efforts they have to expend and the mental pressure they have to bear are far greater than male teachers, and more than they can imagine. They have to sweat a lot harder than their male counterparts. That is why most women teachers choose the first or second option.

B. *Ideological conflict.* Traditional ideas are shackling women teachers' career growth. Lin Yu-tang has described the expectations toward women in the male subculture: "Someone had said that a model wife is a women with new knowledge but old morals." We carried out a survey on the "views and expectations of the spouse." Of the women students polled, 61.7 percent felt their spouses should have stronger careers than themselves while 66.5 percent of the male students hoped that their wives would do better than themselves in taking care of the household. This to a certain extent reflects the potential tendency of the women being willing to be behind men in career and the views of the educated population in today's China toward gender division of work in the home. These traditional role perceptions are ingrained in the minds of students through education. This includes, for instance, stories in elementary and secondary school textbooks of "weak women and strong men," "gentle women and stalwart men," and renowned and great people and leaders who are mostly male. Such one-sided role education gives girls the impression that men are superior to women and gives them a weak sense of societal role and social responsibility. They are therefore not competitive. In family education, parents are always saying "no" to girls. After marriage, the traditional ideas of many female students do not weaken but even strengthen due to family influence. Most men are faced with a contradiction after getting married. On the one hand, to make ends meet they have to support their wives' societal participation; on the other, they worry that they would lose so-called masculine dignity if their wives become more successful than they are and do less housework. This contradictory mindset often puts their wives in a dilemma. When the latter pursue, establish, and enjoy independent careers and lives, the husbands become insecure and set up all kinds of restrictions on their wives. The men especially hate the housework they have to share at home. To them, the home is the woman's business; they therefore chastise their wives for being selfish, not caring about their families, and having no maternal instinct.

A societal role requires women teachers, like male teachers, to enter whole-heartedly into their careers. When career and the family clash, and the demands of society and family correspond with the women's inner moral and ethical values, the women teachers often feel guilty. To gain mental equilibrium, they partly or wholly sacrifice their careers to become good wives and mothers.

C. *Psychological conflict.* Vestiges of Chinese feudal ideas by and large exist in the thinking and minds of women teachers. One manifestation is feelings of inferiority. In China, traditional Confucian ethics forcibly put women in a humble position. The concept that "men are superior to women" is more deeply ingrained in the minds of women than men, and they actually think it a virtue to believe that. Their feeling of inferiority in intelligence is reflected in the very small number of female students or graduates who enroll in graduate school. They feel inferior in work. Far fewer women than men participate in teaching and research competitions. They are willing to take supporting and inferior roles. They have inferior willpower and lack the ability to withstand obstacles and difficulties. This leads to loss of self-confidence, dejection, and depression, all of which put strong pressures on their minds, affect their intelligence, disperse their energy, and suppress their potential. Women also are dependent on other people. At home, they rely on their husbands. When their jobs become a problem, they always sacrifice themselves for their husbands. In society, they rely on the country and the organization, hoping to get sympathy and special consideration. This makes them lack the will to make progress, erodes their potential intelligence and creativity, and eventually causes them to negate their own independent character. Finally, they are mentally weak, as manifested mainly in a lack of ideals, complacency, weak willpower, emotional fragility, and lack of toughness and pioneering spirit in work.

The societal role of women requires a strong motivation, an enterprising spirit, and a sense of responsibility. It asks them to have firm willpower, plenty of energy, and persistence, and to be undaunted by setbacks. To win respect, women should, like men, use their talents and abilities to create values recognized by society. When societal demands conflict with women teachers' mental impediments, the majority of them lose confidence and retreat.

THOUGHTS ON THE OCCUPATIONAL ADJUSTMENT AND DEVELOPMENT OF FEMALE GRADUATES

How can female students in teachers schools proceed steadily and smoothly to a society that awaits them, be competent in future teaching, and develop themselves better? This author thinks that we should pay attention to their occupational adaptability and promote their development when the girls are still students. First, the curriculum should be changed. At present, the new three-year curriculum in teachers schools includes about 25 percent electives (including both limited and free electives). The schools can follow the requirements for teachers in rural secondary education in the twenty-first century and use the teacher training programs of advanced countries as reference to find out the strengths of women in teaching and the individual factors affecting their occupational adaptability; and then reform the curriculum course to strengthen occupational training in these electives. At the same time, the traditional education practice should be changed through the establishment of new types of teaching and practicum to implement plans for training occupational adjustability. Schools can also establish organizations and occupational interest groups composed mainly of girls to effectively improve girls' occupational adjustability.

Second, women teachers should be guided to "negotiate the three hurdles" in order to gain real knowledge. In a society where competition is very sharp, only a girl with knowledge and skills can establish her career. Smart and talented girls need not worry that they can never experience love. Women teachers with families should consider the more important question of their work and not put the lion's share of their attention on husbands and children, or pin their hopes on the latter. In light of their family and career's specific! conditions, they should make timely adjustments as to where to direct their energies and balance their career and home rationally and scientifically. To do this, they must establish the correct outlook on life and be clear about their own goals, and on this basis continuously improve themselves and go forward. In the course of practice, they should never become complacent because of success or dejected due to failure. They should acquire healthy and lofty emotions and feelings. After setting goals, they should constantly temper their willpower and perseverance in practice.

Third, women teachers should be helped to acquire a sense of the mission and social responsibility of the time. This is the source of their strength to become truly talented. They must have a strong wish to be successful in their work and become truly talented professionals and constantly seek motivation for achievement.

(This article resulted from the "Study of Measures to Promote the Occupational Adjustability and Development of Female Students in Normal Schools " under the World Bank's Teachers' Educational Development project.)

(Editor-in-charge: Gu Guanhua)

PART V: TEACHERS' IMPACT ON STUDENTS

In: Chinese Women and the Teaching Profession
Editors: Julia Kwong and Ma Wanhua

ISBN 978-1-59033-916-9
© 2009 Nova Science Publishers, Inc.

Chapter 11

A STUDY ON TEACHERS' GENDER ORIENTATION IN TEACHER/STUDENT INTERACTION

Zhang Lili

Department of Education, Beijing Normal University, China
[Note: Li Lihua, Fan Yong, and Lei Jun participated in this study]

ABSTRACT

A survey of 99 teachers was carried out to examine teachers' perception of the learning abilities of boys and girls, and their behavior in teacher/student interaction. The study found that the respondents believed that male students were better than female students in science courses, and that male abilities in abstract reasoning, creativity, critical thinking, problem detection and problem solving were superior to those of female students. On the other hand, female students were stronger than male students in linguistic expression, literature, imagination, memory, and study habits. Most of the respondents maintained that there was no obvious difference between boys and girls in terms of interpersonal skills, self-confidence, and observation ability. They also maintained that girl students performed better than boys in elementary school, but male students surpassed girls in secondary school, and that girl students had less potential than male students. The study also found gender bias in teacher/student interaction. For example, teachers reminded students that "boys should behave like boys; and girls, like girls." They advised girls to study the humanities and boys to study science. Many teachers were not aware of gender bias in themselves and in textbooks. Based on the views held by the respondents, the study puts forward suggestions for improving gender inequities.

Keywords: Teachers, gender differences, orientation

BACKGROUND TO THE STUDY

The study shows that gender bias exists extensively in all aspects of teaching and education - in textbooks, teacher/student interactions, extracurricular activities, parents' expectations, and others. (Note 1) Other empirical studies have also shown extensive gender bias in textbooks and teacher-student interaction. (Note 2) Others have shown that teachers hold different expectations of, and give different support to boys and girls. (Note 3) A clear evidence of this is the higher dropout rate among girls in economically backward regions. The thinking that males are better than females and that women are inferior to men is still in people's thinking. As a result, discrimination against females continues despite repeated bans as seen in the abandonment of female infants, laying off women from work, lack of women participation in government, difficulties in finding work among female college graduates, and other such practices. The study has found that gender stereotypes among today's college students are similar to those in traditional society. (Note 4) Other empirical studies have also found that junior middle school students and college students all tend to exaggerate the mental differences between males and females, (Note 5) and believe that males have more qualities that lead to achievement. Studies conducted abroad on teacher-student classroom interaction have also shown that teachers have different expectations of male and female students and give them different feedback, (Note 6) that the interaction pattern increasingly disadvantaged female students as they move to higher levels of education, and that girls clearly have fewer opportunities for interaction in maths and science courses than male students. Feminist theory shows that gender concepts are built on the structure of gender inequities that exists extensively in all aspects of social life. Hence, the gender orientation of teachers is tied to gender bias in mainstream society, and passed on to students in the latent curriculum that affects their academic development.

This study attempts, by means of a questionnaire survey, to expose the latent gender orientation and biases in teachers, to understand how such biases are formed, and to offer specific strategies for changing such biases.

METHOD OF STUDY

The respondents of this study are teachers participating in the Masters of Education and other post-graduate programs in the Department of Education, Beijing Normal University. One hundred and ten questionnaires were distributed in May, 2002, and 99 questionnaires were returned with a response rate of 90 percent. Forty-three (43 percent) of the respondents were male teachers, and 56 (57 percent) were female teachers. These teachers came from different types of schools: 13 percent from elementary schools, 60 percent from secondary schools, 14 percent from secondary technical schools, and 8 percent from junior colleges. Among these, 75 percent of the subjects were teachers, 15 percent were school principals, and 8 percent were counselors and other administrative staff. These teachers specialized in the humanities, science, and management.

Preparing the questionnaire went through two stages. In the first phase, eighty-one elementary and secondary school teachers in Qinhuangdao, Hebei province were asked an open-ended question: "Name the differences between male and female students in academic performance." They identified seven dimensions – way of thinking, study methods, character traits, study motives, interests, constraining factors during growth, and ability. These seven aspects arrived at by induction were used to explore the teachers' latent gender orientation. In the second phase, the researchers set up a focus group with three former secondary school teachers to bring together the research results of the previous phase. They reflected on their experiences in teaching that corresponded with these dimensions. On this basis, we designed our interview questions. The questionnaire covered three aspects: personal information, eleven multiple-choice questions, and three open-ended questions. The multiple-choice questions tapped the teachers' views on female students' potential and academic performance, and their views on gender. SPSS statistics software package was used to analyse the quantitative data while textual analysis was used to analyse the open-type questions. Quotations in the following text were taken from answers in the open-ended questions to reflect the respondents' thoughts and feelings.

STUDY RESULTS

1. Teachers' Assessments of Female Students' Academic Performance and Potential

The questionnaire first inquired into the teachers' views about female students' learning potential and academic performance, and the results are shown in table 1. About 75 percent of the respondents believed that female students performed better than male students in elementary school; only 6 percent believed that female students performed better that male students at the secondary level. Some 40 percent believed that female students were inferior to male students in secondary school while about 54 percent maintained there was no difference between their performances in secondary school. Their views of the learning potential of female students were similar to their views on the academic performance of these students. About half of the teachers believed that male students were better than female students, almost another half believed there was no difference among them, and only 2 percent of the respondents believed that female students were better than male students in the high school.

Table 1. Teachers' Views on Female Students' Academic Performance and Potential

Question	Better Than Boys Number (%)	Inferior to Boys Number (%)	No Difference Number (%)	Total Number (%)
Girls' Elementary School Performance	73 (75.3%)	24 (24.7%)	0 (0%)	97 (100%)
Girls' High School Performance	6 (6.2%)	39 (40.2%)	52 (53.6%)	97 (100%)
Girls' Learning Potential	2 (2.0%)	49 (50.0%)	47 (48%)	98 (100%)

2. Teachers' Views on Learning Abilities of Male and Female Students

The respondents maintained that there were various degrees of differences among male and female students in the fourteen abilities cited in the questionnaire. Table 2 shows that over half of the teachers believed boys were better than in girls in six learning abilities. Specifically, between 58 and 85 percent of the teachers judged boys to be better than girls in these six qualities, and only seven percent or less believed girls were better.

Table 2. Teachers' views on differences between boys and girls: Aspects in which boys are better than girls

Question	Boys better number (%)	Same number (%)	Girls better number (%)	Total number (%)
Science ability	84 (84.8%)	13 (13.1%)	2 (2%)	99 (100%)
Abstract thinking	83 (83.8%)	14 (14.1%)	2 (2%)	99 (100%)
Creativity	75 (75.8%)	23 (23.2%)	1 (1%)	99 (100%)
Critical thinking	62 (62.6%)	30 (30.3%)	7 (7.1%)	99 (100%)
Problem solving	61 (63.5%)	33 (34.4%)	2 (2.1%)	96 (100%)
Problem discovery	75 (58.2%)	38 (38.8%)	3 (3.1%)	98 (100%)

Table 3 shows that about half to more than half of the teachers (48 to 78 percent) maintained that female students were stronger than male students in five respects - verbal expression, humanities, imagination, memory, and study habits. The percentage of teachers who believed that boys were superior to girls in these five respects ranged from 4 to 13 percent.

Table 3. Teachers' views on differences between girls and boys: Aspects in which girls are better than boys

Question	Girls better Number (%)	Same Number (%)	Boys better Number (%)	Total Number (%)
Linguistic ability	77 (77.8%)	17 (17.2%)	5 (5.1%)	99 (100%)
Literary thinking	64 (64.6%)	31 (31.3%)	4 (4.0%)	99 (100%)
Imagination	53 (54.6%)	31 (32.0%)	13 (13.4%)	97 (100%)
Memory	50 (50.5%)	40 (40.4%)	9 (9.1%)	99 (100%)
Learning discipline	47 (47.5%)	43 (43.4%)	9 (9.1%)	96 (100%)

Table 4. Teachers' views on differences between girls and boys: Aspects in which there are no differences

Question	Girls better than boys Number (%)	No difference Number (%)	Boys better than girls Number (%)	Total Number (%)
Self-confidence	18 (18.2%)	61 (61.6%)	22 (20.2%)	99 (100%)
Social skills	43 (43.4,%)	47 (47.5%)	9 (9.1%)	99 (100%)
Observation	37 (37.4%)	40 (40.4%)	22 (22.2%)	99 (100%)

Table 4 shows that the respondents believed there was no difference between boys and girls in three respects – self-confidence, interpersonal skill, and ability to observe. The percentage who maintained that there was "no difference" between girls and boys in these respects was higher than the percentages of those who chose either "boys better than girls" or "girls better than boys." Table 4 also shows that 43 percent of the respondents maintained that girls were better than boys in interpersonal skill, while only 9 percent maintained that boys were better. Also, the percentage of those who chose "girls better than boys" in observation was higher than those who chose "boys better than girls."

Chi square test further shows that there was a clear gender difference between the views of male and female teachers in the self-confidence of students ($x2=6.697$, $P<0.05$) As shown in Table 5, the percentage of male teachers who believed that boys were more confident than girls was twice as high as the percentage of female teachers who held the same view, and the percentage of female teachers (57 percent) who saw no difference between boys and girls was far higher than the percentage of male teachers (36 percent) who subscribed to this view.

Table 5. Male and female teachers' confidence in boys and in girls

	Boys better than girls Number (%)	No difference Number (%)	Girls better than boys Number (%)	Total Number (%)
Male teachers	25 (58.0%)	15 (35.0%)	3 (7.0%)	43 (100%)
Women teachers	18 (32.0.%)	32 (57.0%)	6 (11.0%)	56 (100%)
Total	43 (43.4%)	47 (47.5%)	9 (9.1%)	99 (100%)

3. Teachers' Gender Awareness

Table 6 indicates that 25.8 percent of the teachers liked boys more than girls, 15.5 percent liked girls better than boys, and 59 percent maintained that the numbers of boys or girls among their favorite students were about the same, or that they were not aware of any difference between boys and girls. About 31 percent of the female teachers admitted that there were "more boys than girls" among their favourite students, while only 9 percent said that there were "more girls than." Also, 20 percent of the female teachers were not aware of any difference between male and female students. Chi square test shows no significant difference between male and female teachers in this respect ($x2=5.74$. $P>0.05$).

Table 6. Gender of Students Most Liked by Teachers

	Male teachers Number (%)	Female teachers Number (%)	Total teachers Number (%)
More boys than girls	8 (19.0%)	17 (30.9%)	25 (25.8%)
More girls than boys	10 (23.8%)	5 (9.1%)	15 (15.5%)
More or less the same	19 (45.2%)	22 (40.0%)	41 (42.3%)
Unaware of differences	5 (11.9%)	11 (20.0%)	16 (16.5%)
Total	42 (100%)	55 (100%)	97 (100%)

Table 7 indicates that approximately 68 percent of the respondents maintained that female students faced more difficulties than male students in their development with only 7 percent of the surveyed believed that there were more factors unfavorable to male students' development. Table 7 also shows that a higher percentage of male teachers (18.6 percent) than female teachers (12.7 percent) believed that society provided equal opportunities to both; and a lower percentage of male teacher (62.8 percent) than female teachers (72.7 percent) believed that girls faced more unfavourable conditions than boys in their development. However, chi square test shows no significant difference in the views held by male and female teachers in this area ($x2=1.395$, $P>0.05$).

Table 7. Teachers' Views on Development Opportunities For Boys and Girls

	Male Teachers Number (%)	Female Teachers Number (%)	Total Teachers Number (%)
Equal Opportunities	8 (18.6%)	7 (12.7%)	15 (15.3%)
More Unfavourable for Boys	3 (7.0%)	4 (7.3%)	7 (7.1%)
More Unfavourable for Girls	27 (62.8%)	40 (72.7%)	67 (68.4%)
Never made Such Comparison	5 (11.6%)	4 (7.3%)	9 (9.2%)
Total	43 (100%)	55 (100%)	98 (100%)

Table 8 shows that the majority of teachers accepted girl students who regularly went on excursions and played ball games with male students. Teachers who could not accept such behaviour accounted for only 6 percent of those surveyed, and only 1 percent found such girls entirely unacceptable. Chi square test shows no significant gender difference among teachers views on this matter ($x2=2.60$, $P>0.05$}).

Table 8. Teachers' views on girls who go on excursions and play ball games with boys

	Male teachers Number (%)	Female teachers Number (%)	Total teachers Number (%)
Acceptable	25 (58.1%)	37 (67.3%)	62 (63 3%)
Fairly acceptable	14 (32.6%)	15 (27.3%)	29 (29.6%)
Unacceptable	4 (9.3%)	2 (3.6%)	6 (6.1%)
Completely unacceptable		1 (1.8%)	1 (1.0%)
Total	43 (100%)	55 (100%)	98 (100%)

The questionnaire also asked: "If a boy and a girl talked back to you, as a teacher who would you be more angry with?" Over half of the teachers were equally angry with the boy and the girl, but a much higher percentage of female teachers was more angry at the girls (30.9 percent) than at the boys (3.6 percent). Table 9 shows that an equal percentage of male teachers (21 compared to 23 percent) chose the replies: "more angry at boys" and "more angry at girls." Chi square test shows a significant gender difference on this matter between male and female teachers; the difference was significant at the 0.05 and 0.01 levels ($x2=8.86$. $P<0.05$). In other words, female teachers were more likely to be angry and found it more unacceptable if girls talked back at them.

Table 9. Male and female teachers' attitudes towards students who talked back

	Male teachers Number (%)	Female teachers Number (%)	Total teachers Number (%)
More angry at girls	9 (20.9%)	17 (30.9%)	26 (26.5%)
More angry at boys	10 (23.3%)	2 (3.6%)	12 (12.2%)
Equally angry at both	24 (55.8%)	36 (65.5%)	60 (61.2%)
Total	43 (100%)	55 (100%)	98 (100%)

There were two other questions in the questionnaire that measured gender bias and behavior. These concerned the advice teachers gave students on the choice of humanities or science courses. The first situation was a teacher advising a boy with good performances in both disciplines; and in the second, the boy was replaced by a girl. Table 10 shows the advice given by teachers according to their gender. A high percentage of teachers advised the boy to take science courses; among these, 51.2 percent of male teachers and 37.5 percent of female teachers did so. Only a small percentage (5 percent) advised him to take humanities. Chi square result shows no significant gender difference among the teachers ($x2=1.86m$ $p>0.05$)

Table 10. Male and Female Teachers' Advice to
Boys on Choice of Science or Humanities

	Male teachers Number (%)	Female teachers Number (%)	Total teachers Number (%)
Advise him to choose humanities	2 (4.7%)	3 (5.4%)	5 (5.1%)
Advise him to choose science	22 (51.2%)	21 (37.5%)	43 (43.4%)
Let him make his decision	19 (44.2%)	32 (57.1%)	51 (51.5%)
Total	43 (100%)	55 (100%)	98 (100%)

Table 11 shows the advice given to a girl by those surveyed. Approximately one third advised her take humanities, far higher than those advising her to take science. Chi square test indicates no significant gender difference between male and female teachers ($x2=1.11$, $P>0.05$) in the advice given to the girl student.

Table 11. Male and female teachers' advice to girls on choice of science or humanities

	Male teachers Number (%)	Female teachers Number (%)	Total teachers Number (%)
Advise her to choose humanities	15 (34.9%)	16 (28.6%)	31 (31.3%)
Advise her to choose science	8 (18.6%)	8 (14.3%)	16 (16.2%)
Let her make her decision	20 (46.5%)	32 (57.1%)	52 (52.5%)
Total	43 (100%)	55 (100%)	98 (100%)

The question "Do you frequently admonish the students that boys should behave like boys and girls should behave like girls?" was used to examine teachers' gender orientation and behavior in teacher/student interaction, and the results are shown in table 12. About half of the respondents sometimes admonished the students in this way; 11 percent frequently did so, and 8 percent always did so. Chi square test reveals no significant gender difference in the behavior of male and female teachers ($x2=3.59$, $P>0.05$).

Table 12. Frequency with which male and female teachers' remind students: "Boys should behave like boys and girls should behave like girls"

	Male Teachers Number (%)	Female Teachers Number (%)	Total Teachers Number (%)
Always	4 (9.3%)	4 (7.1%)	8 (8.1%)
Often	5 (11.6%)	6 (10.7%)	11 (11.1%)
Sometimes	22 (51.2%)	27 (48.2%)	49 (49.5%)
Occasionally	3 (7.0%)	11 (19.6%)	14 (14.1%)
Never	9 (20.9%)	8 (14.3%)	17 (17.2%)
Total	43 (100%)	55 (100%)	98 (100%)

4. Open-Ended Questions

The first open-ended question in the questionnaire provided a case study – "Li Xia was a good and hardworking student with excellent marks from the time she entered elementary school. To improve her performance for the secondary school entrance examination, she worked even harder and as the best student in her school was accepted by a key senior middle school. Do you think she will be able to maintain her good performance in senior middle school? Explain your reasons using the science subject as an example." Qualitative and quantitative analyses of the answers show that about half of the respondents believed that Li Xia would maintain her performance, 25 percent believed she would not be able to do so, and another 16 percent said it was impossible to predict because of too many unknown factors. The main reasons for believing that Li Xia would not live up to her previous standing were: "Senior middle school science courses require more logical thinking than in junior middle school, and the strategies used in junior middle schools have no relevance at the senior high level"; "The fact that there are more boys in science creates the belief among girls that they cannot do as well as boys in science, and this lowers their self-confidence"; "Junior middle schools attach greater importance to memorizing. Senior middle schools, on the other hand, attach greater importance to abilities of comprehension and inference. A person with good memory does not necessarily have good comprehensive powers. Boys are better than girls in maths, physics, and chemistry"; "It will be very difficult for her to maintain her excellent performance, because she has relied on hard work and her learning abilities may not be able to keep up with the new demands." Others felt she would maintain her standard because of her hard work, discipline, and her good foundation. Those who cited too many unknowns pointed out: "Hard work and industry may make up for her shortcomings"; that it would be necessary to "exclude extrinsic factors, such as [the traditional belief that] lack of talent is a virtue in girls, the sexual temptations of puberty and so forth."

The second open-ended questions was: "Do you believe gender bias exists in today's teaching materials? Please explain and give examples." The results in table 13 show that 55.6

percent of the teachers believed there was no gender bias in teaching materials, 35.6 percent maintained there was some gender bias, and 9 percent would not provide an answer.

Table 13. Teachers' Views on Gender Bias in Teaching Materials

	No bias Number (%)	Some bias Number (%)	Cannot say, never thought of it Number (%)	Total Number (%)
Male	7 (47,0%)	6 (40.0%)	2 (13.0%)	15 (100%)
Female	18 (60.0%)	10 (33.0%)	2 (7.0%)	30 (100%)
Total	25 (55.6%)	16 (35.6%)	4 (8.9%)	45 (100%)

The last open-ended question attempted to find out teachers' opinions and suggestions in improving gender inequity. An analysis of the replies given by male and female teachers is given below.

Replies by the male teachers are divided into the following six categories:

1) No changes should be made. They believed that "the difference between genders cannot be eliminated, and there is no discrimination against females to speak of. There is no inequity in teaching. Boys and girls have equal access to education. As for what will happen after education-let society resolves such issues."

2) Changing teachers' behavior. Specific strategies were proposed, such as: "Do not strengthen the gender stereotype by saying that certain things may be done by boys and certain things may be done by girls"; "Teachers or parents should not evaluate gender differences and behavior of their students"; and "Give girls students more opportunities to do hands-on work, to think, and to ask questions, and give boys more opportunities to think in overall terms and attend to details." There were also proposals to develop mental health education and to de-emphasize gender differences through physical labor, sports, guard duty, and other such educational and teaching activities.

3) Systemic changes. Some maintained that society should, as far as possible, provide females with more equitable opportunities for competition and change the procedures of employment. For instance, "The government should actively intervene when employment units refuse to interview girls in recruitment."

4) Reform teaching materials. Teaching materials [should] provide examples of equality between genders and versatility in gender roles.

5) Efforts by females themselves. Some maintained that the key to changing the present situation was for females to achieve their own independence.

6) Changing the gender ratio among teachers. Some maintained that there should be more male teachers: "The number of elementary school male teachers should be increased, and there should be male teachers in kindergartens, so as to shape strong personalities in young children."

The suggestions from female teachers were as follows:

1) No change needed. Some maintained that equality is relative, that "gender difference is an objective fact, and arbitrary talk of equality in education might bring inequity to even more people."

2) Changing the teachers' views on gender. Some proposed training for teaching to change gender perceptions. A few female teachers suggested: "the curriculum should pay attention to the development of both genders, and that boys and girls should participate equally in group activities"; "offer electives to students at different educational levels so children can choose according to their preferences"; "encourage boys and girls to participate in sports and various kinds of social activities" and "organize more activities in which boys can participate."

3) Adjust the teachers' gender ratio. Some maintained "the number of male teachers is low in secondary and elementary schools, and a nanny-type education exists"; "attention should be paid to gender balance among teachers, so that students learn the strengths of both genders, and develop sound personalities. In particular, there are to be more 'uncles' in kindergartens, to expose children to male strength and fortitude"; and "a balance between males and females should be maintained among school teachers, as these will be mutually complementary."

4) Eliminate structural obstructions. "Provide males and females with equal opportunities to broaden their development and refrain from putting up artificial obstructions"; "change people's concepts by means of the media and other ways"; change the thinking that attaches more importance to males than females. Refrain from stereotyping In teaching and training and practise gender equality In social division of work." Some people also proposed using legislation to ensure equal opportunities of employment for both genders and stop discrimination against females.

5) Reform the educational system. Teachers pointed out: "I believe that so long as we do not harbor any bias toward the students, treat them fairly and without discrimination, and do our best to discover their strong points, we will find our students intelligent and lovable, whether they are boys or girls."; "I believe that gender differences in school will be eliminated so long as teachers aim to develop each student and treat each as an individual," and "Education is to help the individual to develop in an all round and sound manner. However, there are differences between boys and girls and we must treat them differently. Boys and girls should all be educated, but we must not place them under the same criteria. It is sufficient if they develop their full potential."

DISCUSSION

The study shows that the respondents believed boys were better than girl in learning science subjects, abstract reasoning, creativity, critical thinking, solving problems, and the ability to discover problems. And girls were stronger than boys in linguistic expression, learning humanities courses, imagination, memory, and study habits. There was no difference between boys and girls in interpersonal skills, self-confidence, and the ability to observe problems. The respondents also maintained that girls performed better than boys in elementary school, but boys surpassed girls in secondary school, and that boys had more potential than girls. The study also found that gender bias in teacher-student interaction. For example: female teachers liked boys better than girls, and were more tolerant of boys who offended them. All teachers, male or female alike, were likely to remind students that "boys should behave like boys and girls should behave like girls," and were likely to counsel boys to study science and girls to study the humanities. The study also showed that some teachers believed that society provided both genders equal room for development and were unaware of the hurdles facing women; some even believed that society was unfair to the development of males.

The above results show fairly strong gender stereotyping among teachers, and that in some respects more bias among female teachers than male teachers. Such gender bias in teachers is translated into different expectations for boys and girls, and such expectations are in turn transmitted to the students through teacher-student interaction. Rosenthal has pointed out that teachers' expectations can become reality. In other words, students sense their teachers' expectation, concern for, and confidence in them, and will develop in the direction the teachers expect them to do; whereas students on whom techers place low expectations will develop comparatively less well. It is clear that the effects of gender bias works as follows:

gender bias-->teachers' different expectations for boys and girls-->expectations translate into realities-->more bias

The way in which gender bias works is like the Matthew effect. First, teachers' gender bias limits girls' development; this becomes a reality which only confirms and increases the teachers' bias; and deepens the gender differences that already exist in real life. As one female teacher said: "Teachers generally believe that girls are more obedient and boys more intelligent, and will unconsciously impose these expectations on their students in their teaching. In such an environment, the students will develop in the direction their teachers expected. A vicious circle results.

This study does not intend to explore gender differences *per se,* but seeks to understand people's comprehension of gender differences, and to understand the deleterious effects of teachers' gender orientation on student development. Fiske & Stevens have pointed out that gender stereotyping has the following characteristics: (Note 7)

1. Effects of cultural norms. Traditional norms require that females "should" be such and such.
2. Restriction of their privileges. Men are dominant in society, and the number of females in professions of high social status is proportionately small.
3. Women experience isolation. The lack of females in many professions has implications for women in these professions. For example, women scientists and women city mayors are regarded as unique, and society has set ways of looking at them.
4. Sex and physiology. When choosing a spouse, females seek resources and protection, whereas men look for a spouse to procreate.
5. Extreme views are hidden in modern society. Equality is a basic ideal in modern society. This, to a certain extent, prevents extreme views on gender from surfacing and gender bias is therefore concealed.

Chodorow also opposes the essentialist view on gender differences, and maintains that gender characteristics are formed in social life and gender differences are socially constructed. (Note 8) Self concept emerges in the child's growing up process. Because the mother assumes major responsibilities in raising children, girls feel a greater affinity to their mother while boys have a greater sense of difference. This causes boys to develop greater independence and self-determination, whereas girls are more nurturant. Although Chodorow's theory is psychological, she emphasizes the social construction of gender differences and especially the important effects of mental state, society, and culture on gender development.

According to Chodorow's theory of gender development, the forming of gender characteristics is shaped by one's interactive relationship and by the environment. If one is to change women's unfavorable situation, one should transform the attitudes and behavior of teachers. To transform teachers' attitudes and behavior is to understand and reflect on this bias. This study indicates that teachers lack sufficient gender awareness and even believe in "basic" gender differences. In other words, they believe in absolute gender differences. A male teacher stated in his answer: "Gender differences inevitably give rise to many differences in mental ability, behavior, and roles. The existence of such differences is an inevitable reflection of gender differences; they are normal, and cannot be eliminated. The awareness of human concern may be enhanced in teaching,... but there is no need to emphasize absolute equality between men and women. If one is to insist on absolute equality, one must first eliminate the physiological differences and have men give birth to children. Or, it can be achieved only after the differences of sex no longer exist in the world." Such views show how some teachers reject gender issues, and tell us that the transformation of gender concepts is no easy matter. It will require that we devise, through practice, effective strategies for intervening in and influencing that process. As a respondent said, one should "help teachers understand physical and mental development in boys and girls, recognize that no essential differences exist between them, especially there is no significant difference in their intelligence. From there, we proceed to transform the differences in teachers' expectations on boys and girls." For this purpose, the present study has devised a set of participatory-type teachers' training activities. It is hoped that this program will be perfected in practice and give impetus to teachers' concern for gender issues.

REFERENCE MATERIALS

[1]   Wu Kangning: *The Sociology of Education;* People's Education Publishing House, 1998. Edited by Lu Jie and Wu Kangning; People's Education Publishing House, 1990.

[2]   Topical report (s) on studies of gender analyses in teaching materials [?].

[3]   Zhou Wei and Lu Jin (ed): *Hope Amid Poverty: Education for Girls and Women in the Impoverished Regions of West China,* Guangxi Education Publishing House, 1997.

[4]   Qian Yiming, Luo Shanhong et al: "A Preliminary Investigation into Stereotyped Gender Impressions"; Applied Psychology (Hangzhou), January 14-19, 1999.

[5]   Zhang De: "Investigation Report on Gender Bias," carried in *Psychology – Materials from Newspapers and Periodical Copied by People's University,* no. 2, 1991.

[6]   Good, T.L. & Brophy, J.E. (1997). Translated by Wu Wenzhong: *Classroom Studies;* Wunan Books Publishing Company (Taiwan); pp. 37-38.

[7]   Fiske, ST. & Stevens, I.E. (1998): "What's so special about sex? Gender stereotyping and discrimination"; in Clincy, B. & Norman, J. (Eds.), *The Gender and Psychology Reader* (pp. 505-522).

[8]   Chodorow, N. (1998). Feminism and Difference: "Gender Relation, and Difference in Psychoanalytic Perspective"; in Clincy, B. & Norman, J. (Eds), *The Gender and Psychology Reader* (pp. 383-395).

In: Chinese Women and the Teaching Profession
Editors: Julia Kwong and Ma Wanhua

ISBN 978-1-59033-916-9
© 2009 Nova Science Publishers, Inc.

Chapter 12

THE EFFECTS OF TEACHER-STUDENT INTERACTION ON THE DEVELOPMENT OF GIRL STUDENTS' PERSONALITY

Li Lihua

Institute of Education, Beijing Normal University, China

ABSTRACT

This paper explores how teachers' gender bias affects their attitudes and ways in teacher-student interaction, and thereby adversely affecting the healthy development of girls. I have focused my survey on teachers because they have an important influence on girls; and I believe that an effective way of resolving the problem is to eliminate gender biases in teachers to give girls equal opportunities to education. Huang Shufen, director of the Department of Compulsory Education of the Ministry of Education, has said, "Neglect of female in education is a glaring problem. We should pay more attention to it and make improvements because the predicament of females delays their development and also human development as a whole." Hence, how to effectively eliminate teachers' gender bias and to create an environment that supports equal growth and development for girls and boys in school should be regarded as a major topic of exploration.

I. EFFECTS OF TEACHERS' GENDER BIAS IN TEACHER-STUDENT INTERACTION ON THE DEVELOPMENT OF GIRLS

Symbol interaction theory maintains that "teacher-student interaction is a quantitatively and qualitatively differentiated process depending on the individuals involved." In this process, teachers exhibit varying degrees of bias for or against students. The choice of subjects, content, length, and structure of the relationship in interaction differ from person to person. These differences in interaction result in different personality development and performance among students, and can even lead to unequal social development. In teacher-student interaction, teachers' gender bias makes them believe that girls are basically inferior to boys, e.g., boys are more logical and have more personal qualities that lead them to professional success. They believe that girls should have gentleness, quiet demeanor, kindness, and other such personality traits acknowledged by tradition, and should assume traditional social roles e.g. raising children and managing household chores. Teachers bring with them these gender-biased opinions in their interaction with this special group of persons – girls, and place them in a disadvantaged position compared with the boys. In other words, teachers harbor different expectations for boys and girls. These gender-biased expectations of the teacher are subconsciously manifested in their speech and action. Because teachers occupy a position of authority in the students' minds, their utterances and actions imperceptibly shape the girls' gender perception, and have a particularly major effect on the formation and development of girls' personalities.

1.1. Influences on Girls' Self-perception, including their Self-awareness, Self-evaluation, Self-adjustment, and Behavior

To understand how teachers' gender bias affects girls' personality development, we designed a "gender and education" survey questionnaire. The subjects were 110 masters of education students taking classes in Beijing Normal University, and 99 questionnaires were returned. A case was presented in the questionnaire: "Li Xia was a good and studious pupil with excellent marks from the time she entered elementary school. To improve her performance for the secondary school entrance examinations, she worked even harder and, as the best student in her school, was accepted by a key senior middle school." The question was: "Do you think she will maintain her good performance in senior middle school? Explain your reasons, using science courses as an example." Among the 99 returned questionnaires, 16 percent was uncertain, and 25 percent maintained that it was not possible for her to do so. The reasons given were, without exception, as follows:

1) Senior middle school physics and chemistry courses are difficult, and girls generally cannot compete with boys
2) Most girls have no potential at the senior middle school level.
3) To achieve in junior middle schools requires only a fairly good memory. Senior middle schools, on the other hand, require fairly strong abilities of comprehension and inference; and boys possess such qualities. Therefore it is difficult for most girls to maintain excellent performances in the senior middle school.
4) The fact that there are more boys in science classes creates pressure for girls to believe that girls are not as good as boys in science, and this lowers the girls' self-confidence.

Even the 59 percent who answered in the positively expressed some uncertainty, "Yes they can, but they must put in more efforts than boys," and "Yes, they can, but they cannot depend on memorizing." As girls constantly get messages from their teachers that they are not as good as boys in science, or that they are not suited for such courses, they will lose confidence in their intelligence, lose self-respect and have low self-evaluation. We found in our interviews that teachers frequently asked boys to solve the more difficult problems. In so doing, the teachers show high hopes in the boys, give them more opportunities to cultivate courage and determination to overcome difficulties, and more confidence. Most girls, however, have no such opportunities. Yet determination is only developed in the course of constantly overcoming difficulties, and only by overcoming difficulties can one develop one's wisdom and talent, and achieve. Thus most girls entertain doubts in their own abilities when they face difficulties in study, and are unlikely to harness the same courage and confidence as boys in overcoming difficulties; but willpower is sometimes the magic weapon to overcome difficulties and gain success.

Historically, females existed as appendages to males in patriarchal society, and women in China and abroad did not have equal access to education as men. Although women as a group has acquired the right to be educated in the same schools as men in modern society, even in a developed nation like the United States, women were only admitted to Oberlin College only in the 1930s. The courses offered them were not rigorous and they were required to serve male students and do their laundry. Generally, girls find themselves surrounded by the gender bias in textbooks and in their teachers' behavior – a powerful educational environment that often makes them feel incapable. It is indeed difficult for girls in such an educational environment to develop the same self-confidence as boys. Also, the beliefs that women's minds are not as agile as men's, and are not suitable to work in fields long dominated by men have hampered their development and the realization of their worth. They are stereotyped the moment they enter this world, and lose the opportunity for equal development with males. Even if women have extraordinary abilities in fields dominated by men, it is likely that these potentials – that might have made them surpass these men – be stifled by these socially acknowledged fetters before they become adults.

1.2. Effects of Gender Bias in Teacher-Student Interaction on Girls' Future Ideals, Beliefs, World Outlook, and Interests

Some believe that interests are inherent and cannot be cultivated and or changed. This view is incorrect. Although congenital factors play some part in the formation of interests, postnatal guidance and training are more important. However, many successful persons did not pursue their first interests. Their accomplishments were the result of patient nurturing by their schools, teachers, and parents; and the development of lofty ideals based on this foundation.

So, what suggestions for future gender roles do girls get from teachers in teacher-student interaction? Or shall we say, what kind of ideals, beliefs, and interests do teachers unconsciously set up for these girls?

In the following game, for instance, the girl who plays the mother grasps the back of a chair and runs around the room as if she is driving a car. Another girl goes up to the teacher and says: "Teacher, she does not know how to be a mother. She is making a mess of the home." The teacher asks: "What should mothers do?" The other girl replies: "Mothers don't run around driving cars." The teacher says approvingly: "Right, a mother cooks dinner. She tidies the rooms, sweeps the floor, and tells stories to her children. She also goes out shopping for groceries. Look how untidy your house is! Nobody comes any more!" In this game, the teacher unconsciously orients the girls to their future gender role of doing household chores. Similar influences accumulated over the years till adolescence – an important time in the formation of world outlook, ideals, and beliefs, make it impossible for girls to undergo same development as boys. Most girls acknowledge the future social role conferred on them by teachers who embrace traditional customs and habits. This lowers the girls' ideals, beliefs, and goals. They do not pay attention to developing lofty interests and hobbies, independence, creativity, or initiative in an all-round manner. Such deficits in their personality make it difficult for them to realize their own worth in society in future, and they will exist only as appendages to males. Thus the females' sense of emptiness and loss is perpetuated.

1.3. Effects of Gender Bias in Teacher-Student Interaction on Girls' Personality Traits – Temperament, Capabilities, Emotions, and Feelings

During our interviews, we found many teachers believe that boys should protect girls (even in primary school). For example, teachers frequently remind boys to look after girls, to let the latter get on the bus first, and to carry their knapsacks on field trips. The teachers want is to protect the girls. In the long run, this creates the image of girls as less capable than boys, dependent on others, and needing care. At the same time boys acquires higher stature.

How do teachers' gender-bias during teacher-student interaction affect girls' emotion and feeling?

"Emotion and feeling" refer to people's attitudes toward objective matters or subjects. For example, some things make people joyful and happy; others make people depressed or sad. Some things make people disgusted or angry; and others elicit people's admiration and love. Gender bias causes teachers to convey different emotion and feeling to boys and girls in their interaction and, consequently, causes boys and girls to experience different emotion and feeling. We found in our interviews that if girls constitute the majority of good students in the first and second years of senior middle school, the home room teachers will worry about admission rates to colleges and universities, because they fear that the girls will not maintain their good performances. Such worries are undoubtedly displayed in teacher-student interaction, and at such times the teachers are conveying a lack of confidence in the girls, apprehension, and even expressions of anxiety. These negative emotions are bound to affect the formation of healthy and happy emotions in the girls. Another manifestation of inequality is that teachers regard any decline in girls' performance in senior middle school as natural and to be expected. Not so with boys. The teachers lavish greater attention and encouragement on the boys and convey to them confidence and positive feeling. This "Pygmalion" effect helps the boys to overcome their negative emotions and adjust their mental state to conquer difficulties and secure success. All these make the boys experience more of the emotions and feelings needed for success.

II. ELIMINATE TEACHERS' GENDER-BIASED PERCEPTIONS AND CREATE A SALUTARY TEACHER/STUDENT INTERACTION ATMOSPHERE FOR GIRLS' ALL-ROUND DEVELOPMENT

Girls' future development depends on full development of their potential. Hence, how to eliminate teachers' gender bias; how to get rid of such obsolete concepts from China's traditional culture, such as, "men are measured by their talent and women, their beauty" and "men should be strong and women should be like flowers;" how to create in schools an educational atmosphere where boys and girls are treated equally; how to eliminate factors unfavorable to personality development in girls; how to cultivate independent personalities based on self-respect, self-improvement, and self-esteem; and how to create favorable conditions for girls' future development – all deserve attention, I therefore propose:

2.1. prestigious research institutions should design training programs to make teachers aware of the dangers inherent in such biases and adopt the appropriate attitude and behavior toward boys and girls in teacher-student interaction; and equality towards boys and girls should be manifested in verbal exchanges between teachers and students;

2.2. intervention training be conducted for girls to encourage them to develop appropriate self-appraisal, self-confidence, and especially an awareness of opposing traditional gender roles to lay the foundation for their future development;

2.3. traditional formulations on gender differences in teaching materials be changed and replaced with the newest research results (for example, the discipline educational sociology should present the newest results of gender studies in China and abroad, and in particular the research findings of the Americans, such as, MacCoby, Jacklin, and M. C. Linn, so that the new generation of teachers develop a scientific and equitable gender awareness; and

2.4. eliminate gender bias in the media and especially from school textbooks, so that society may have a broad and correct understanding.

In sum, teachers have the responsibility to provide girls with equal opportunities for development in their interaction in school classes. They have the responsibility to create a salutary environment for the healthy development of girls' personalities and to lay a solid foundation for the social development of girls who make up half of the world's population. Only thus can one improve the human course of development.

REFERENCE MATERIALS

[1]   Wu Kangning: *The Sociology of Education;* People's Education Publishing House, 1998; p. 39.

[2]   Zheng Xinrong et al: Fu jiaoyu ye shehui xingbie (Endow Education with Social Genders); p. 160.

[3]   Song Hui: "Who Are Good Students?"; Gender Analyses of Teaching Materials, 2001.

[4]   Chen Qi et al: Dangdai jiaoyu xinlixue (Contemporary Sociology of Education); Beijing Normal University Printing House, p. 277.

PART VI: PROPOSED STRATEGIES

In: Chinese Women and the Teaching Profession
Editors: Julia Kwong and Ma Wanhua

ISBN 978-1-59033-916-9
© 2009 Nova Science Publishers, Inc.

Chapter 13

ON THE AWARENESS OF HOME ECONOMICS AMONG WOMEN TEACHERS AND OTHER STAFF MEMBERS IN HIGHER EDUCATION[*]

Zhang Xiuqing

ABSTRACT

Strengthening women teachers and other staff members' awareness of home management has major significance in raising the status and enriching the role of women in society and the home in the new period. This article describes the author's views on how to reinforce this awareness among women teachers and other staff members in higher educational institutions.

FOR WOMEN TEACHERS AND OTHER STAFF MEMBERS IN HIGHER EDUCATION TO GAIN AN AWARENESS OF HOME ECONOMICS IS THE NEED OF THE TIMES

The reform of China's economic system and development of the socialist market economy provide women great opportunities for social participation in different areas. An increasing number of women are utilizing their intelligence, talent, and creativity on the job and, shoulder to shoulder with men, are writing a glorious chapter in lie annals of building socialism with Chinese characteristics. However, the position and function of women in society, especially in the home, is no something other family members can replace. The family is a cell of society, and in present-day society women comrades who shoulder the dual responsibilities of the family and a career not only need to achieve in their work but also to play an important role at home. Hence it is even more necessary for women comrades to have

---

[*] Translation © 2000 M.E. Sharpe, Inc., from the Chinese text. Zhang Xiuqing, "Shilun gaoxiao nujiaozhigongde jiazheng yishi," *Liaoning shifandaxue xuebao (shekeban)* (Liaoning Teacher University Bulletin, Sociology Section), no. 1, 1993.

an awareness of home economics; this is the need of social development and the need of the four modernizations. What is a fitting paradigm for a modern family? With the upsurge of reform and opening, it is time to update old, outdated ideas of the home. Most contemporary families with members working in higher education are families where both husband and wife are intellectuals, and probably both professors, both associate professors, or both lecturers (or of equivalent professional titles). Both spouses usually have equal educational credentials and similar professional titles. In families with such high academic credentials, women comrades are politically and professionally on a par with men. A realistic issue that cannot be ignored in these modem families is how intellectual women can play a major role, comply with the needs of modem social development, and fully take on their role as "half the sky." Forming an image of the women of the new period is urgent. Enrichment of family life and the constant rise in living standards, the rapid development of modern science and technology and the in-depth progress of reform and opening doubtlessly put the family in modern society at a high starting point. Hence, a family in modern society should not be solely a living unit, but an all-round family. Only so can it keep up with the pace of the times and gradually conform with the new situation of reform and opening. This is the reason why highly specialized women teachers and other staff members in higher education must have an awareness of and training in home economics.

HOME ECONOMICS IS REQUISITE FOR WOMEN TEACHERS AND OTHER STAFF MEMBERS IN HIGHER EDUCATION

Home economics is a comprehensive discipline that focuses on research in family life. It has a big influence on family happiness and social development and brings blessings to mankind. Its contents can roughly be divided into: Taking care of home chores, waiting upon husbands, rearing children, cooking, fashion design, tailoring, sewing, home decoration, environmental sanitation, and family and social public relations. In other countries, especially Japan, home economics has become a requisite course in the life of women.

Chinese women have the virtues of oriental women. They are educated in traditional mores from childhood. After marriage, the majority are capable of taking charge of household matters, waiting upon their husbands, and bringing up children. This type of traditional family in which the "man takes care of matters outside the home and the woman takes care of matters inside the home" has continued for thousands of years in China. With the progress of civilization and the liberation of women, they leave home to work in society and increase their self-worth. Taking care of home chores is now shared by husband and wife. However, with the rapid development of society and the further rise in women's social position, some women comrades, especially those in higher education with great professional accomplishments, are no longer satisfied with being only "dutiful wives and good mothers." This trend has especially gained strength after reform and opening and women feel that they "cannot live tied to the sides of men." Even those who are willing to be dutiful wives and good mothers feel that they would like to do more. Because modern families demand high levels of culture, knowledge, and management, they need to have an atmosphere of education, living, learning, and career. In this situation, a "dutiful wife and good mother" needs to learn home economics.

What, then, is the kind of "dutiful wife and good mother" who meets the demands of a modern family? A "dutiful wife" should be someone who truly trusts, understands, and supports her husband and goes ahead hand in hand with her husband in their careers. A "good mother" should never be confined to feeding and fattening her children and doing everything for them. Some parents fear their children will not pass the examinations to enter senior high or college, and feed them "chicken, fish, meat, eggs, chocolate, and even queen bee honey." They neglect the training of their physical and other non-intellectual abilities, to the point that these "little emperors" cannot tell one kind of grain from another and are lazy. They are completely ignorant of the knowledge needed by modem society. This shows that tremendous energy has to be expended to bring up children. Because of the narrow scope of their knowledge which is insufficient to cope with the urgent problems of the day, many families can only tighten their belts and economize on expenses so that they can hire tutors for their children. These steps are important, but the improvement of the parents' own quality should not ignored. Therefore, modern women comrades have to learn home economics to become more versatile so that they can gradually meet the needs of the modern family.

We oppose the feudal idea of "dutiful wife and good mother" but not the "dutiful wife and good mother" of modern society. Home economics requires modern "dutiful wives and good mothers" not merely to wait on their husbands and educate their children but, more importantly, to be worthy assistants to their husbands in their work, discuss research projects and techniques, and encourage each other in their careers. Strong women of the new period should have stronger abilities than men at work and be "dutiful wives and good mothers" at home. The female author Chen Rong said: "To talk about family chores does not lower the dignity of a woman. I take exception to some female comrades, especially female intellectuals, who proudly claim they don't know how to cook." This is also the case in countries abroad. In England, former Prime Minister Margaret Thatcher would get groceries after work to make delectable food for her husband at home. This is not something that a maid or a chef can replace; it has to do with emotions, emotions that cannot be replaced by someone else. This is family.

For love, for life, for family happiness, and for career, women comrades not only must have an "awareness of home economics" but must learn it well. This is especially important to women in higher education, because most of them are career women and have heavy teaching and research workloads. How to make up the lesson (they missed) in home economics is an important issue.

MEASURES TO FOSTER AWARENESS OF HOME ECONOMICS

To enhance the awareness of home economics on the part of women teachers and other staff members in higher education, we must consciously uphold the principle of dialectical materialism, which says that the external cause is the condition of change while the internal cause is the basis of change, and that the external cause can only be effective through the internal cause. We must earnestly start from the following concepts.

First, women teachers and other staff members should be educated to truly understand the importance of home economics and the need to learn it. Since it is a comprehensive discipline that brings human happiness, all society should attach importance to such education. Home economics should be included in the movements for "good mothers," "good wives," and "five good families," to improve women's awareness and thus fundamentally improve their social position so that they would try to become strong women of the "trail blazing," "independent," and "intellectual" type.

Families of intellectuals in higher education need to have a higher degree of civilization. Financially, we may not for the moment become millionaires, but in spiritual civilization we must become billionaires. We should follow a timetable during work, and should scientifically follow a timetable at home as well to create a good home environment. To be a good homemaker is like leading a work unit—explaining how things should be done, giving emotional support, and being a role model to educate the children and influence the husband—so that a new type of family emerges.

Second, women should constantly study and adjust their thinking. Marxism holds that the final emancipation of humankind rests in the emancipation of the female sex, and the fundamental thing about women's complete liberation rests on liberating their consciousness. The 1990s is a critical period for the realization of China's general strategic goal of socialist modernization. With the development of modern mass production, many new things, new knowledge, and new problems have appeared, causing changes in people's habits, ideas, and ways of thinking and speeding up the pace of life.

To keep pace with the times and be able to rationally, conscientiously, and effectively participate in the revolution, study is a must. The special position of women comrades determines their special function in modern families. New contents should be injected into the criteria of a new, modern family. Homemakers should have an awareness of home economics and make up this lesson. Only so can their ability to manage the home comply with the needs of reform and opening. Home management must coordinate with the rest of society. Home building must conform with social development. Women comrades, whether from the perspective of culture or ability, must be guided by new ideas and a new awareness—that of home economics.

(Editor-in-charge: Guo Changzheng)

In: Chinese Women and the Teaching Profession
Editors: Julia Kwong and Ma Wanhua

ISBN 978-1-59033-916-9
© 2009 Nova Science Publishers, Inc.

Chapter 14

ON WAYS TO STRENGTHEN THE TEACHING ROLE OF WOMEN TEACHERS – SURVEY AND ANALYSIS OF FEMALE TEACHERS AT SICHUAN UNIVERSITY

Liu Xuanqing
Sichuan University, China

ABSTRACT

This paper analyses data from a 1998 survey of female teachers at Sichuan University to explore and to seek ways to strengthen their role in institutions of higher learning. The author found that female teachers taught an average of 1.124 class hours in 1998, equivalent to a teaching load of 5.65 hours per week; but the number of courses taught by women declined as one moved to the senior levels with 54.48 percent of those surveyed teaching basic theory, 40.0 percent teaching specialized ones, and 17.97 percent teaching technical or methodological courses. This distribution suggested that lack of specialized skills might be the chief hindrance to their professional advancement, and their low participation rate in research – only 27.58 percent – the basic reason for their lack of appropriate professional skills.

Key terms: Women teachers; Teaching role; Lecturing frequency

In the 50 years since the founding of New China [People's Republic of China], a fundamental change has occurred in the economic and social status of Chinese women with the introduction of the state policy to promote "equality between men and women." The number of women taking part in social and economic activities has increased greatly, and so has their contribution. The gender-blind social domain of higher education especially provides excellent opportunities for women's active participation. As a result of their collective efforts, women employees in China's institutions of higher learning has reached 37.2 percent, and the percentage of women in full-time employment in these institutions has reached 30.9 percent.[1] In a few key colleges and universities, the number and percentage of women staff are even slightly higher than the national average.[2] The percentage of Chinese women in higher education has reached between 30 and 40 percent; this is a great achievement for women's emancipation and social progress in China. However, it is not enough to simply increase their representation in higher education. We must understand their professional role and explore ways to enhance, consolidate, and improve their position in today's increasing competition when redundant staff are forced off or have to change jobs. If this is not done, it will be difficult to increase their representation in higher education, and their numbers may even decline. For this reason, this article uses data gathered from a survey of female teachers in Sichuan University conducted in 1998 to examine and to explore ways to enhance their role in teaching in institutions of higher learning.

I. SURVEY RESULTS

Teaching is one of the two basic functions of institutions of higher learning; and this work is mundane compared to research. The teaching load of female teachers reflects the use they made of their specialized skills. Courses offered by universities can be divided into three categories — basic courses, specialized courses, and technical basic courses (jishu jichu ke). Our questionnaire was designed with these three categories in mind. However, there was a high non-response rate in the 169 returned questionnaires for the questions on the types of courses taught. For instance, 89 respondents in our sample did not provide information on whether they were teaching basic courses, 110 did not answer the question on specialized courses, and as many as 143 missing responses were found for the question on technical basic courses. That is, 52. 66 percent of the respondents failed to reply to whether they taught basic courses, 65,09 percent failed to reply whether they taught specialized courses, and 84.62 percent failed to reply whether they taught technical basic courses. The high percentage of missing responses makes it difficult to analyze the distribution of courses taught by female teachers.

Table 1. Number of respondents teaching basic courses

	Missing Response	Yes	No	Total
Number	89	79	1	169
Percentage	52.66	46.75	0.59	100

Why did so many female teachers not answer this question? After studying the survey results, we interpret the non-response of the women teachers as a negative reply. This is because the number of non-response added to answers containing a "yes" or "no" totaled 169, the number of returned questionnaires. Table 1, for example, shows that among the 169

---

[1] China Statistical Yearbook, China Statistics Publishing House, 1933 ed., p. 14.

[2] For instance, according to a survey conducted by the Women's Research Center of Wuhan University (Wuhan University Women's Research Center: Women and Society; Wuhan University Publishing House; June 1996 ed.), between 1991 and 1994, women accounted for 40 percent of the university staff, and female accounted for 31 percent of its teaching faculty.

returned questionnaires, 89 respondents made no reply, 79 replied "yes," and only 1 answered "no," and these added up to 169, the number of returned questionnaires.

Similarly, we find as many as 110 missing responses, 58 positive responses and one negative response, totaling 169, in the distribution of responses to the question on teaching specialized classes. The same distribution is found with the question on teaching technical basic courses. The 142 missing responses, 26 "yes" answers, and 0 "no" reply came to exactly 169, the total number of returned questionnaires. Clearly, this pattern with the number of non-response and the number of those who responded equal to the number in the sample happening three times is not coincidental. Clearly, we did not make the instruction clear to the respondent. As a result, all the respondents (except one who clearly understood to give a negative reply) believed that a non-response was equivalent to a negative reply. The person who correctly understood the instruction has taught only technical basic courses but not basic nor specialized courses; so there was one negative reply to each of the former two questions and no negative reply for the last one. If our interpretation is considered reflective of the actual situation, we can re-compile the results of the survey into a table that looks as follows:

Table 2. Courses taught by female staff in Sichuan University

COURSES TAUGHT	YES	NO	TOTAL
Teach Basic Courses	79(46.75%)	90(53.25%)	169(100%)
Teach Specialized Courses	58(34.32%)	111(65,68%)	169(100%)
Teach Basic Technical Courses	26(15.38%)	143(84.62%)	169(100%)

II. ANALYSIS OF THE TEACHING ROLE OF FEMALE TEACHERS

Now we can interpret the teaching load of female teachers and staff from the table, but first we have to take out the full-time administrative and Party personnel from the sample. Our results have shown that among our sample, 9 persons were trade union cadres not involved in teaching and another 13 were unit heads. Another 4 were faculty or departmental level cadres who did not state whether they taught full-time or part-time. If we assume that half of them were not full-time teachers, then there would be 24 non-full-time teachers and 145 full-time teachers in our sample. Based on these figures, Table 2 can be revised as follows:

Table 3. Courses taught by female teachers at Sichuan University

COURSES TAUGHT	YES	NO	TOTAL
Teach Basic Courses	79(54.48%)	66(45.52%)	145(100%)
Teach Specialized Courses	58(40.0%)	87(60.0%)	145(100%)
Teach Basic Technical Courses	26(17.93%)	119(82.07%)	145(100%)

What does this table tell us? In our analysis, the first thing we found was – female teachers taught an average of more than one course per person. Among the 145 female teachers surveyed, 79 persons taught basic courses, 58 persons taught specialized courses, and

26 persons taught technical basic courses, totaling 163. In fact, some female teachers taught basic and specialized course, or even a technical basic course, while others did not teach any course at all. On average, the 145 female teachers together taught courses 163 times — a per capita average of 1.124 courses per person. In other words, each person on average taught more than one course. If we look at this figure using the university criterion of requiring a person to teach four to six class hours per week, or an average of five hours per week, then we can see that a female teacher at Sichuan University carried an average teaching load of 5. 62 class hours per week. Whether this work load meets the expectation for the teaching position and requirement (ding gang ding bian) depends on the nature of classes being taught.

Secondly, the number of the classes taught by female instructors declined with increase in the difficulty of the courses. Basic courses teach basic theory and methods. Since the development of science and technology is relatively slow and teaching materials are readily available, teaching these courses is less difficult than teaching specialized or technical basic courses. Specialized courses are the core courses for students in various areas of specializations; they provide students comprehensive and in-depth understanding of, recent developments, and research methods in the discipline. The textbooks available do not adequately reflect these rapid developments and changes, so the instructors have to supplement the teaching materials from their own research. This requires from the teachers fairly deep understanding in science and technology. Technical basic courses bridges basic and specialized courses, These are the main avenues for students to learn basic skills and hands-on abilities. This requires the teachers to have a relatively extensive knowledge base. One can see from the above table that the number of female teachers teaching these courses at Sichuan University declined as we moved from basic to specialized to technical courses – from 54.48 percent teaching basic courses, to 40.0 percent teaching specialized courses, finally to 17.93 percent teaching technical basic courses. This progressive decline indicates that females teachers have two problems – lack of in-deep theoretical understanding, and lack of breadth in specialized skills. Resolving these problems, especially broadening the specialized skills of female teachers, would significantly increase their role in teaching. This is our second observation in examining the role of female teachers.

Third, a basic way to improve their theoretical understanding and broadening their specialized skills is to encourage them to participate in scientific research. To do this, the first step is for them to enrol in post-graduate programs and study for higher academic degrees. In their fulfilment of courses requirements and preparation of their graduation theses, they can significantly improve their academic standards. Given the limited space available in graduate programs, a more effective way to do so is to encourage them to undertake scientific research. It is precisely in this area that female teachers displayed a low participation rate as compared to their teaching. The survey showed that only 14 person/times were participating in state-level [research] projects, 12 person/times in provincial-level projects, and 2 person/times in municipal-level topics. They totalled 40 person/times, a very small percentage of the 145 total respondents. That is, female teachers taught an average of more than one course per person, but three fourths of them did not participate in any scientific research. This was our third major observation from our analysis. Such a low participation rate in research is clearly unfavorable to broadening their theoretical understanding and improving their specialized skills. The key to increase women's professional role in institutions of higher learning is to encourage them to participate in scientific research.

Four. Mentoring will substantially increase female teachers' participation in scientific research, and enhance their role in teaching. Our record showed that 3 persons participated in the Sixth-Five-Year-Plan research projects, 9 persons in the Seventh-Five-Year-Plan research projects, 26 persons in the Eighth-Five-Year-Plan research projects, and 18 persons in the Ninth-Five-Year-Plan research projects. The growing numbers of women participating in these projects suggest that with the deepening of educational reforms and increasing competition in universities female teachers face increasing pressure to raise their theoretical understanding and skills. However, women will face great difficulties in these endeavours, and will take a long time to develop if left on their own. Mentoring should be used wherever conditions permit to produce quick results. I make this suggestion because the survey shows that the age structure and characteristics of female teachers are suitable for that. The survey indicates that the 20 to 30 age group, the largest cohort among Sichuan University's female staff, accounted for 29.95 percent of the respondents; the 31 to 35 age group accounted for 18.34 percent. Together they made up 48.29 percent or nearly half of the female staff. These women teachers under 35 have little work experience and hold low professional ranks. But they are energetic and adaptive. Clearly, mentoring can quickly and effectively help female teachers with these characteristics to improve their specialized skills. Middle-aged and older female teachers should pass on their knowledge, help, and set examples for young teachers especially in applying for, taking responsibilities in, and carrying out research projects. This practice would very much help the younger teachers in designing research projects, understanding the requirements for applications, learning the application process, implementing the research project, and improving their research abilities.

Finally, encouraging male teachers to mentor female teachers is an important way to increase the professional role women played on campus. Although the survey found that female teachers in the 55 to 60 age group made up 15.98 percent of the respondents, they were near retirement and could not be mentoring young female teachers for long. Female teachers aged 51 to 55 constituted only 10 percent of the respondents; their number would clearly be inadequate to mentor young female teachers who made up almost half of the women teachers. Female teachers of the 46 to 50 age accounted for a mere 3.55 percent of the total, they were mainly worker-peasant-soldier graduates of the Cultural Revolution era and would have difficulties mentoring their younger colleagues. Although the 36 to 45 age group of younger female teachers made up 20 percent of the respondents, they had to improve themselves and would be unlikely to mentor effectively. In sum, implementing the mentoring system within the ranks of female teachers is problematic and presents many difficulties, and it is also unnecessary to restrict mentoring to within the women group. Generally speaking, male teachers are far ahead of female teachers in their teaching and research achievements, both quantitatively and qualitatively. Female teachers' sensitivity in comprehension and observation complement such deficiencies in male teachers; and research teams made up of both male and female teachers should be a good way to mentor young female staff and to produce good research results. Hence, giving full play to the potential of male teachers in mentoring young women faculty members in research is worth considering because this practice can quickly and effectively improve female teachers' research and teaching capabilities.

Conclusion

A survey of the professional role of female staff at Sichuan University have shown that female teachers undertake an average of more than one course per person, but the number of courses taught declines with increases in the difficulty of these courses. By contrast, female teachers play a relatively small role in scientific research with only slightly more than one fourth taking part in research projects of various levels. This may be the major reason why female teachers teach few and only lower level specialized and technical courses. The remedy is for them to participate actively in research to improve their theoretical understanding and broaden their technical skills. With almost half of the women teachers lacking experience but adaptive, a quick and effective way of improving their theoretical understanding and technical skills is to encourage experienced senior teachers to mentor them in designing, applying for, and participating in research projects. Also, considering the age structure and research level of female teachers, it is necessary to involve male teachers in mentoring young female teachers to help them to rapidly enhance their professional role in institutions of higher learning.

In: Chinese Women and the Teaching Profession
Editors: Julia Kwong and Ma Wanhua

ISBN 978-1-59033-916-9
© 2009 Nova Science Publishers, Inc.

Chapter 15

A Tentative Discussion on the Achievement Consciousness of Women Teachers in Institutions of Higher Learning

Wan Qionghua

Department of Political Law, Hunan Yueyang Normal Institute, China

Abstract

Women teachers in institutions of higher learning are relatively highly educated among China's educated females. They are also a growing force in China's higher education. But their professional achievements fall far behind their male counterparts and put them in a disadvantageous position in higher education. This article uses the perspectives of achievement orientation and gender analysis to propose the creation if a socio-cultural environment beneficial the development of consciousness of self-affirmation among female college students and the development of university women teachers. This will also be beneficial to higher education and gender equality in society.

Keywords: Women teachers in institutions of higher learning; achievement orientation; gender

In the wake of the development of higher education, the number and ratio of women among the teachers in China's institutions of higher learning are steadily growing. More and more educated women are participating in higher education, a professional domain once dominated by men; and they have become an important new force in the development of higher education. Women university teachers have a relatively high educational level among the country's professional educated females. They are in a certain sense the role model and representative of women in that their achievement motivation and professional accomplishments subtly affect other women. However, studies of these women have been overlooked. I believe that examining achievement orientation and its manifestations among university women, and analyzing the factors that affect their achievement consciousness are important for eliminating unfavorable socio-cultural factors in their physical and mental health development, and to encourage them to play a more active role in higher education and social development.

I. ANALYSIS OF WOMEN'S SUBJECTIVE CONSCIOUSNESS AND ACHIEVEMENT ORIENTATION

Womens' subjective consciousness is an important topic in women's studies. It lays the theoretical foundation for a lifetime of struggle and achievement for women. Women's subjective consciousness is the conscious awareness of women as subject, of their position, role, and value in the objective world[1] Specifically, it is the women's ability to recognize and fulfill their historical mission, social responsibilities, and duties in life: to recognize their own qualities, to participate in an unique way to change society, and to affirm and fulfill their needs and values. It is the basis of women's initiative and self-determination. It is also the source of their creativity and a rational point of departure of women identification of their own value.

Women's subjective consciousness is a broad concept. It is an abstract concept in the network of concepts, and its contents are manifested in three levels: 1) Subjective determination. This means the subject is conscious of her independence from extrinsic forces and freely controls her own activities. Subjective determination requires a positive attitude toward life and motivation. Women can possess subjective consciousness only if they have a deep understanding of themselves and give full play to their personalities. 2) Achievement orientation. This refers to the conscious recognition on the part of the person as subject of the ideals and behavior that must constantly be achieved and created. [Note 1. p. 23] It is composed mainly of achievement motivation, objectives of self-development, and a degree of concern for the surrounding. Achievement orientation is the "compass" that drives women in their development and is an important manifestation of their self-respect and self-improvement. 3) Consciousness of all-round development. The mind and heart of the modern person must be in harmony and he or she possesses mental qualities developed in an all-round manner. Only when women have the consciousness of all-round development can they create new knowledge, adapt to social needs, and make adjustments.

Among the three levels of subjective consciousness, awareness of self-determination is the base, and achievement orientation is the motive force. The latter determines the direction of one's actions. However, self-determination and achievement orientation only point to the possibility and direction for women's development, they need a consciousness of all-round development to answer the question as to how women should grow and develop. In sum, the three complement one another, and form the sequential links of a continuous chain.

---

[1] Wei Guoying: *Nu xing xue gai lun* (A General Discussion on Women's Studies); Beijing; Beijing University Publishing House, 2000, p. 23.

II. ANALYSIS OF THE ACHIEVEMENT ORIENTATION OF WOMEN TEACHERS IN INSTITUTIONS OF HIGHER LEARNING

1. Expectations of Achievement in Work (i.e. Achievement Motivation)

A person's expectation shapes his or her achievements. Generally speaking, the higher the expectation, the greater the achievement; and vice versa. The Chinese-Canadian "Women's Participation in Higher Education" research group gathered statistics on male and female teachers in 11 institutions of higher learning in various areas, and on 180 female and 214 male teachers at a certain institution of higher learning. The results showed that male teachers of all ages entertained higher expectations than female teachers, and their professional achievements and ranks were higher than females'. The research group concluded from their analysis that the relatively low expectation entertained by university female teachers from their work is the biggest factor affecting their participation in higher education.[2]

The "low achievement orientation" among university female teachers makes us think. Society does not place emphasis on women's intellect and leadership abilities, but encourages them to develop social skills.[3] This tendency in society is subtly manifested in speech and action, and the expectations of countless people are translated into women's personal expectations. In a study of women's IQ and motivation quoted by Yuan, he found that the higher men's I.Q, the higher their expectations; but conversely, the higher women's IQ, the lower their motivation. Women's motivation changes in inverse ratio to their IQ.[4]

2. Development Objectives

A person's orientation or view of self-development is most important for one's career. In recent years, Chinese womens' view of their value in life is a cause for anxiety. They have turned from their former focus on personal development to a focus on marriage. This has brought about an enormous change in the way they position themselves. Instead of improving oneself to become successful, many women now want to be "dutiful wives and good mothers" centered around the life of men. This social phenomenon will no doubt affect the development objectives of women teachers in institutions of higher education.

In a survey of 110 male teachers and 127 female teachers at Tongji University on the subject "Views of Female Teachers in Institutions of Higher Learning on Marriage, Family, and Career," Pan Xiudi found that 43.63 percent of women teachers agreed with the statement: "The wife gains honor from her husband's success, and marrying well is better that working well"; 60.17 percent of women teachers believed that: "If it would give my spouse a better future in his career, I would sacrifice my own career." It is therefore not surprising that 17.9 percent of the women viewed supporting their husbands' work and 26 percent viewed housework and educating children as their "main preoccupation."[5] These women are willing to

---

[2] Ibid, p. 96.

[3] Yuan Zhenguo et al: *Nan nu chayi xinlixue* (Psychology of Male-Female Disparity); Tianjin: Tianjin People's Publishing House, 1989, P. 251.

[4] Ibid, p. 251.

[5] Wei Guoying, p. 22.

sacrifice themselves transferring their initiatives and dedication for their own career to those of their husbands' so as to realize their own values through their husbands' success, some even maintain that "my husband's successes are my successes." Social psychologists label this consciousness in women "modern sense of achievement" (shidai chengjiu gan). This displaced achievement among women teachers will widen the professional gap between themselves and their husbands. The effect will be felt in the family, social interaction, and gradually in the whole society, thus adversely affecting womens' fulfillment of their own values, and resulting in the gap between the professional achievements of the two genders.

The survey also showed that some woman teachers in institutions of higher learning are afraid of success. They are even more afraid of the isolation, misunderstanding, and reproaches brought on by success coming from their colleagues, families, and society. Men's success, however, brings them a sense of accomplishment, satisfaction, and praise; whereas with women, success brings fear, misunderstanding, sarcastic comments, and even family break-up. A survey of women teachers in 34 institutions of higher learning in Hubei province, Zhu Pingyan et al asked women "What do you seek in your profession?" About 11.5 percent replied "I only seek to fulfill my responsibilities." About 8 percent did not have any goals in "objectives of personal development,"; about 23.9 percent rated their "self-evaluation of work achievements" as passable and 0.6 percent rated themselves as "not too good." [Note 5. p. 58] When woman teachers were asked, "Do you feel any conflict between family and professional development?" in Pan Xuidi's survey, 22.22 percent and 42.74 percent respectively replied "frequently" and "sometimes." And when asked the question "In general, what would be your choice?" 13.16 percent of the respondents chose "I place more importance on the family," 58.77 percent chose "I give equal attention to the two."[6] In a survey I conducted on 276 women teachers at the Yueyang Normal Institute of Hunan Province, I asked "What is important for women?" Only 9 persons (or 7.2 percent) of the women teachers chose "career," and as many as thirty persons (or 24 percent) of all the respondents did not pick "career" at all from the choices given. These surveys show that women teachers in institutions of higher education do not set high goals for their own development. The idea of "getting a man as insurance" is still the choice for many women. Hence, "a strange trend is happening in China's current stage of development. Acquiring an education is an indispensable means to attain womens' independence and self-improvement. But even women with higher education do not necessarily choose the path of self-improvement and independence."[7]

III. Factors Affecting University Women Teachers' Achievement Orientation

In the wake of the international women's movement, Western feminism has found that socially created gender rather than physiological gender is the cause of inequality and career disparity between men and women. Socialization is the process whereby individuals learn

---

[6] Pan Xiudi: *Gaoxiao nu jiaoshi hunyin, jiating yu shiye* (Marriage, Family, and Career among Women Teachers of Institutions of Higher Education); *Rencai fazan* (Talent Development), 2000, (7), p. 22.

[7] He Qinglian: *Zhongguo funu diwei bianhua de shehui huanjing fenxi* (Analysis of the Social Environment for Changes in the Status of Chinese Women); Guilin; Lijiang Publishing House, 2001, p. 126.

gender roles and their limits; this gender identification runs through a person's lifetime, and structures gender relations.[8] No doubt, the growth of women teachers in institutions of higher learning is also a process of gender role socialization. The socio-cultural environment leaves a deep imprint on their consciousness, and in turn affect their achievement orientation.

1. Parents' Influence on the Forming of Children's Gender Roles

Some researchers maintain that the earliest and most important factor in gender socialization is the family and the influence exerted by parents. Parents shape children's behavior in line with society's gender expectation. A child's gender is determined from birth. Parents use every opportunity to instill into the child the concept that "boys and girls are different." Parents' education for boys emphasizes the attainment of success and control over one's emotions, whereas girls get more love and affection. In general, parents want boys to be courageous and girls to be obedient. Boys develop their courage when they are rewarded by their parents for bravery and criticized for being meek and docile. Girls develop obedience when being praised for submissiveness and admonished for independent behavior. The cumulative and subtle effects of parents' different treatments of children in the family lay the initial foundation in the socialization of their children's gender roles, and affect their achievement orientation.

2. Gender Bias in School Education

School education plays an enormous role in every person's growth and development, and gender socialization. Many researchers have found that gender bias in school education hampers the development of girls' self-confidence.

First, character portrayal in teaching materials subtly propagates the idea that "males are the center" and "girls are inferior to boys." Gender analyses conducted by scholars on China's secondary and elementary school language texts have found that men appear more often than females in secondary and elementary school language teaching materials (males account for 81 percent and females, 19 percent), and these women are portrayed for the most part in their traditional roles.[9]

Secondly, teachers treat boys and girls differently. In the mid-1980s, researchers abroad spent three years observing over a hundred classes and found that both male and female teachers more frequently asked boys to answer questions and gave them more encouragement than girls. When a girl gave a wrong answer, the teacher frequently asked other students to help them; but when a boy gave a wrong answer, the teacher would help and encourage them to find the correct answer.[10] This neglect deprives girls the opportunities to train and show their abilities. American researchers maintain that such gender bias in the teaching process

---

[8] Zheng Xinrong and Du Fangqin: *Shehui xingbie yu funu fazhan* (Social Genders and Women's Development), Xian: Shaanxi People's Education Publishing House, 2000, pp. 26-27.

[9] Shi Jinghuan: *Jiaocai zhong de xingbie wenti janjiu* (As Study on Gender Issues in Teaching Materials); Funu *yanjiu lun cong* (Collected Papers on Womens' Studies), 2000, (1), p. 34.

[10] Zhang Haiyan: *Nuxing zixinxin yanjiu gaisu* (A Brief Account of Studies on Female Self-Confidence); *Shehui xinli yanjiu* (A Study on Social Mentality), 1993. (3). p. 48-49.

engenders a "learned helplessness" in girls (that is, lack of perseverance and loss of confidence).

Thirdly, teachers frequently entertain high expectations on the intelligence, independence, and logical thinking of students with male qualities; but believe that students with typically female qualities will have difficulties in their studies. In sum, the teachers' conscious or unconscious gender bias enhances and encourage greater initiative and more active learning in boys, but have an inhibiting effect on girls' enthusiasm.

3. Gender Bias Created by Cultural Tradition and Habits

The well-known American cultural anthropologist, Margaret Mead, investigated three primitive tribes living in a mountain region, on a river bank, and on the shore of a lake in New Guinea. She showed that people with the same biological characteristics developed different gender norms and behavior in different socio-cultural backgrounds. Mead said, "In light of the materials we have gathered, we can say that in many respects (though not all), the two genders' personality traits have very little to do with sex differences per se, in the same way as the men's and women's dress and behavior prescribed by society at given times have nothing to do with physiological differences."[11] She believes that "culture makes every effort under the most complex conditions to make a newly-born infant grow up according to a given cultural image."[12] In fact, society not only gently reminds children of gender differences, but also provides strict guidelines for the behavior of girls and boys. When the girl is young, parents want her to be a socially acknowledged good girl. When she marries, her husband wants her to be a socially acknowledged good wife; and when she has children, everyone demands that she be a good mother. Good girl – good wife – good mother, such is the females' growth history. Socialization of the female has a dual function. One is to turn women into women needed by society, and the other is to make them the women in society rather than an "individual" among women in society. We can see how language, customs, and habits in social culture influence the socialization of gender roles.

One. The influence of social customs and habits. In China that places so much importance on ceremony and propriety, different rites and treatment are reserved for newly-born boys and girls. The "Book of Odes: Xiao Ya" states: "When a boy is born, he shall sleep on a bed, be clothed in a long robe, and play with a jade tablet. When a girl is born, she shall sleep on the ground, be clothed in a short jacket, and play with a clay spindle." One sleeps on a bed, the other on the floor; one is clothed in a long robe, the other in a short jacket; one plays with a jade tablet, the other with a clay spindle. How obvious is the difference! For thousands of years, such customs and habits have influenced people's attitudes toward boys and girls, and people's expectations of their achievements. Just as the lyrics of a congratulatory folk song say: giving birth to a boy is a "jade occasion" and an "event of full happiness," whereas giving birth to a girl is a "clay occasion" and an "event of partial happiness." Two, the influence of language. Perceptions of gender is imprinted in language as a cultural artifact. The structure (semantics, characters, grammar, words and phrases, etc.) or

---

[11] Margaret Mead, San *ge yuanshi buluo* de *xingbie yu qizhi* (Sex and Temperaments of Three Primitive Societies); Hangzhou: Zhejiang People's Publishing House, 1988, p. 266.

[12] Ibid, p. 258.

social function of language is filled with gender bias. This bias is manifested first in the male norm, or in other words, the patriarchal principle, in a language. Men are regarded as the standard members of society, and this bias is seen in the discriminatory references to females. In inscriptions on bones or tortoise shells of the Shang Dynasty, the character "woman" depicts a figure kneeling on the ground, and the character "wife" is represented by a woman holding a broom. The former shows the lowly status of females, and the latter depicts the woman's main function. The most blatant discrimination against female is the many characters denoting pejorative terms with the "woman" radical on the side or inside the characters, such as the characters for "treacherous," "sycophantic," "jealous," "greedy," and so forth. Three, patriarchal society has fabricated such theories as "female mental retardation," "female lowliness and weakness," and "female attraction of misfortunes" to show the absence or lack of intellectual power in women. The "theory of female intellectual retardation" expounds the view that women are living beings lacking or devoid of intelligence. Precisely because men affirm that women are intellectually handicapped, any indications of intellectual potential in women intelligence are nipped in the bud. The ethical principle enunciated as "women's virtue lies in absence of talent" sets women's virtue in diametric opposition to her talents, and has disregarded or stifled women's knowledge and intelligence for three thousand years. To this day, "women's virtue lies in absence of talent" is still an invisible rule with which men evaluate women and women restrain themselves.

It is evident that the particularities and commonalities of gender roles have the same origin in socio-culture. One might say that Meade's proposition in the 1930s that gender differences are created by social factors is still true today. As Meade said, "Due to the existence of two kinds of social personality – the gender-controlled and gender-limited personalities in a given society, all people born in a society are impaired to varying degrees... . We must seriously take into consideration the many potentials, and should create a less arbitrary social structure to provide an appropriate place for the development of every human potential. ... In this society, the disparities between the individuals' natural endowments will replace man-made disparities. "[13]

IV. THE SIGNIFICANCE OF RAISING THE ACHIEVEMENT ORIENTATION OF WOMEN TEACHERS IN INSTITUTIONS OF HIGHER LEARNING

The development and achievements of women teachers in institutions of higher learning are not only pertinent to the realization of their own worth, but directly relate to the development of women's talent and liberation. As the achievement orientation of women teachers in institutions of higher learning is raised, they will play an active role in higher education and social development.

1. Raising the achievement consciousness of university women teachers will improve higher education. Currently, women teachers account for more than a third of the teachers in institutions of higher learning; their situation will directly affect the

---

[13] Ibid, p. 307.

situation in higher education. "Our higher education will become an effective and well-run system if women play their role well in higher education."[14] In the new century, we have a new understanding of the role of and expectations from the teachers in institutions of higher learning. A foreign study has found that thirty-eight of the factors associated with good teachers have to do with their emotion and personality. A survey of 90 male and female students at Liaoning Normal University on their impressions of teachers[15] shows that women teachers have more "sentimental" traits, such as, kindliness, cordiality, gentleness, sincerity, devotion, than male teachers. They are skilled in using love and affection to bridge communication between teachers and students, and impress their students with high-quality teaching and sincere and caring attitude. They have undoubtedly made unique contributions to higher education and will continue to improve the overall standard of higher education.

2. Raising the achievement orientation of women teachers in institutions of higher learning will enhance self-assertion among female college students. Women teachers who possess independence and self-determination, self-respect and self-confidence; and who have achieved professional status equal to those of men by using their intellect, talents, and industry, are undoubtedly persuasive role models for female college students and help them build their confidence and look for their own worth. The achievement motivation of some female college students in pursuing a career is weakened by the fetters of backward traditional ideas and bias. The traditional concept that "men are stronger than women" continues to prevent them from asserting themselves. They often lack confidence in their own abilities. All these directly affect the development and full expression of the intelligence and aptitudes of female college students. The restoration and strengthening of old social division of labor within the family (men take charge of external matter and women, of household matters) particularly in the last few years has made some college girls to see developing the skills of the "dutiful-wife-and-good-mother" as the main object in college. They give no thought to achievement and resign themselves to mediocrity. A large number of women university teachers establishing their positions both in the family and in society through hard work would undoubtedly point the direction for college girls in terms of shouldering the pressures of their dual role, help them deal with the contradictions between career and family, and overcome the difficulties and perplexities inherent in the "small self" and the seek healthy development of their own personalities.

3. Raising the achievement orientation of women university teachers will promote gender equity in institutions of higher learning and in society. The currently observed gender division of labor in behavior and social structure that makes it hard for women to take part in activities in the public domain is deeply rooted in history. They also prevent men from assuming more duties and responsibilities in the family, such as bringing up the children, caring for the old and sick, and so forth (survey of teachers at Tongji University) found that 64.5 percent of women spent more than two

---

[14] Yuan Zhenguo, op. cit., p. 31.

[15] Zheng Xinrong and Du Fangqin: Shehui xingbie yu funu fazhan (Social Genders and Women's Development), Xian: Shaanxi People's Education Publishing House, 2000, p. 389.

hours doing housework but only 37 percent of male teachers did so.[16] Current discussions on "phased employment" (jieduan juiye, i.e. whether women work depends on their stage in life) and "women going home" show that although the emancipation of women has expanded their responsibilities from "inside the house" to include "taking charge both inside and outside the house;" men have not undergone any fundamental change, they still retain their traditional gender role attitudes and expectations. In the process of the country's economic reform, the pressures of market competition and weakening administrative rules that guarantee women's rights have reactivated gender prejudice and discrimination that have once been weakening. They have brought about, to a certain extent, the re-emergence of the traditional gender culture. Today, we hope that men will also awaken from their erstwhile "glories and dreams" as women gain their consciousness.

Raising the achievement orientation of woman teachers in institutions of higher education will, on the one hand, help to eliminate gender inequities so that women—and men as well—will be liberated from the obsolete patterns of gender behavior. More importantly, this change will arouse the broad masses of women so that they show concern for themselves and for the female community, and struggle in the spirit of self-respect, self-improvement, tenacity, diligence, selflessnes, and fearlessness to establish a new image for the female community so that both genders will together build a society of harmony and co-existence founded upon on freedom.

REFERENCE

[1] Wei Guoying: Nu xing xue gai lun (A General Discussion on Women's Studies); Beijing; Beijing University Publishing House, 2000.

[2] Zhang Xiaohong, Zou Hui, and Zhu Yonghua: Gaodeng jiaoyu zhong funu canyu zhuangkuang de fenxi (An Analysis of the State of Women's Participation in Higher Education); Higher Education Publishing House, 2001, (3).

[3] Yuan Zhenguo et al: Nan nu chayi xinlixue (Psychology of Male-Female Disparity); Tianjin: Tianjin People's Publishing House, 1989.

[4] Pan Xiudi: Gaoxiao nu jiaoshi hunyin, jiating yu shiye (Marriage, Family, and Career among Women Teachers of Institutions of Higher Education); Rencai fazan (Talent Development), 2000, (7).

[5] Zhu Pingyan: Shichang jingjixia zhishi funu de chengjiu yu chaoyue (Achievement and Transcendence by Intellectual Females under a Market Economy); Shehuizhuyi yanjiu (Studies on Socialism); 1997, (3).

[6] He Qinglian: Zhongguo funu diwei bianhua de shehui huanjing fenxi (Analysis of the Social Environment for Changes in the Status of Chinese Women); Guilin; Lijiang Publishing House, 2001.

[7] Zheng Xinrong and Du Fangqin: Shehui xingbie yu funu fazhan (Social Genders and Women's Development), Xian: Shaanxi People's Education Publishing House, 2000.

---

[16] Pan Xiu di, op. cit.,p. 23.

[8]   Shi Jinghuan: Jiaocai zhong de xingbie wenti janjiu (As Study on Gender Issues in
      Teaching Materials); Funu yanjiu lun cong (Collected Papers on Womens' Studies),
      2000, (1).

[9]   .Zhang Haiyan: Nuxing zixinxin yanjiu gaisu (A Brief Account of Studies on Female
      Self-Confidence) [J]; Shehui xinli yanjiu (A Study on Social Mentality), 1993. (3).

[10] Margaret Mead, San ge yuanshi buluo de xingbie yu qizhi (Sex and Temperament in
      Three Primitive Societies; Hangzhou: Zhejiang People's Publishing House, 1988.

[11] Lu Jie: Funu diwei tigao yu zhonguo gaodeng jiaoyu (Improvement of Women's Status
      and China's Higher Education); Gaodeng jiaoyu yanjiu (Studies on Higher Education),
      1995, (4).

INDEX

E

F

S